Everyman's Poetry

Everyman, I will go with thee,
and be thy guide

Ivor Gurney

Selected and edited by GEORGE WALTER

University of Sussex

E
J. M.

This edition first published by Everyman Paperbacks in 1996
Selection, introduction and other critical apparatus
© J. M. Dent 1996

Text © The Ivor Gurney Estate 1996

J. M. Dent
Orion Publishing Group
Orion House
5 Upper St Martin's Lane
London WC2H 9EA

Typeset by Deltatype Ltd, Ellesmere Port, Cheshire
Printed in Great Britain by
The Guernsey Press Co. Ltd, Guernsey, C.I.

British Library Cataloguing-in-Publication
Data is available upon request.

ISBN 0 460 87797 6

Contents

III. October 1922 – December 1924

Note on the Author and Editor

IVOR GURNEY was born in Gloucester on 28 August 1890. The son of a tailor, he showed his talent for music at an early age, winning a place in Gloucester Cathedral Choir in 1900. In 1911, after six years as an articled pupil of Herbert Brewer, he took up an open scholarship for composition at the Royal College of Music. Despite being troubled by the mental illness which was to dog him intermittently for the rest of his life, he had by 1914 produced some of his finest song settings; he had also begun to experiment with poetry. He joined the 5th Gloucester Reserve Battalion in 1915 and saw active service on the Western Front between June 1916 and September 1917. Although trench life did not completely stifle his musical activities, he now wrote prolifically, publishing his first book of verse, *Severn & Somme*, in 1917. He was invalided home after being gassed during the Passchendaele offensive and suffered a severe breakdown in early 1918. Resuming his studies at the Royal College of Music after the war, he published a further collection of his poems, *War's Embers*, in 1919. The next two years were his most creative and successful period but his mental condition was deteriorating and in September 1922 he was committed first to an asylum in Gloucester and then to the City of London Mental Hospital in Dartford. Although able to continue his creative activities over the next decade, he never fully recovered and died of tuberculosis at Dartford on 26 December 1937.

GEORGE WALTER is Lecturer in English in the School of Cultural and Community Studies at the University of Sussex. His other publications include *Ivor Gurney: Best Poems and The Book of Five Makings* (MidNAG & Carcanet, 1995) with R. K. R. Thornton. He is currently producing an edition of Wilfred Owen's poems for the Everyman's Poetry series.

Chronology of Gurney's Life

Year	Life
1890	Ivor Bertie Gurney born at 3 Queen Street, Gloucester, 28 August, the second of four children of David Gurney, a tailor, and Florence Lugg
1890s	Family move to shop premises at 19 Barton Street. Gurney attends National School and All Saints Sunday School
1900	Wins place in Gloucester Cathedral Choir and attends King's School. Begins to learn the organ
1906	Leaves Cathedral Choir and King's School. Becomes articled pupil of Dr Herbert Brewer, organist of Gloucester Cathedral, alongside Herbert Howells and Ivor Novello.
1910	Ralph Vaughan Williams's *Fantasia on a Theme by Thomas Tallis* premièred at the Gloucester Three Choirs Festival in August. Gurney and Howells attend
1911	Takes up scholarship to the Royal College of Music. Taught composition by Charles Villiers Stanford. Begins friendship with Marion. M. Scott, musicologist and secretary of the R.C.M. Union
1912	*Georgian Poetry 1911–1912* published
1913	Begins to write poetry. Diagnosed as suffering from dyspepsia and 'neurasthenia' in May. Writes his settings of five Elizabethan lyrics – the 'Elizas' – during the winter
1914	Britain declares war on Germany, 4 August. Gurney volunteers but is rejected because of defective eyesight. Takes post as organist at Christ Church, High Wycombe, in October
1915	Volunteers again, 9 February, and is drafted into the 5th Gloucester Regiment Reserve Battalion, the '2/5th Glosters'. Spends rest of the year in training
	Rupert Brooke dies of blood-poisoning in the Dardanelles, 23 April
1916	Battalion at Le Havre, 25 May. Moved to Laventie-Fauquissart sector of the Western Front. Sees service at Riez Bailleul, La Gorgue, Neuve-Chappelle, Robecq and

Gonnehem. Battle of the Somme begins on 1 July.
Battalion moves south to the Somme sector in October.
Sees service at Grandcourt, Aveluy and Ovillers.
Transferred to Varennes for training, 30 December
Gurney in Rest Station for 'cold in the stomach' in
December, then takes temporary job with water carts in
Sanitary Section. Returns to normal duties at the end of
the following month

1917   Battalion moved to Ablaincourt sector in February, then
follows German withdrawal to Vermand. Despatched to
Arras front in May, in reserve for Third Battle of Ypres 31
July
Edward Thomas killed at Arras, 9 May
Gurney shot through upper arm, 6 April – Good Friday –
and sent to hospital in Rouen. Back with battalion by 18
May, where he becomes platoon's crack shot. Transfers to
Machine Gun Corps at Vaux. Gassed at St Julien, near
Passchendaele, 10 September, and sent to recuperate in
Edinburgh War Hospital, Bangour, where he meets and
falls in love with Annie Nelson Drummond, a V.A.D.
nurse. Transferred to Northumberland for signalling
course in November. *Severn & Somme* published, 16
November

1918   Examined for effects of gas and admitted to Newcastle
General Hospital in February, moving to convalescent
depot at Brancepeth Castle the following month. Writes
to Marion Scott, 18 March, telling her that he has spoken
to 'the spirit of Beethoven'. Transferred to Lord Derby's
War Hospital, Warrington, in May. Sends suicide note to
Marion Scott in June and tells superiors that he hears
voices and wishes to be sent to an asylum. Sent to
Middlesex War Hospital at St Albans and discharged from
the army, 4 October. Returns to Barton Street,
Gloucester, taking a job in a munitions factory.
Behaviour erratic; makes several attempts to go to sea.
Finishes work in munitions factory on 11 November –
Armistice Day
Wilfred Owen killed on Sambre-Oise canal on 4 November

1919   Returns to Royal College of Music in January. Taught
composition by Vaughan Williams. *Severn & Somme*

reprinted. Back at Barton Street by late February, correcting proofs of *War's Embers*. Working at Dryhill Farm, Shurdington, in April, but back in London by May, when *War's Embers* is published. Submits many poems to journals but none are accepted. Takes post as organist at Christ Church, High Wycombe, in September. Moving in London literary circles

1920 Walks from High Wycombe to Dryhill Farm, via Oxford, in late February. Tries to set up home in cottage at Cold Slad, Dryhill in May but back in London by October. The 'Elizas' and other songs published
Collected Poems of Edward Thomas published

1921 Living with his aunt at Longford, Gloucester, in April. Has songs and piano preludes published but is unsuccessful in attempt to have poems included in *Georgian Poetry 1920–1922*. Finds work on a farm in May and formally leaves the Royal College of Music two months later. Back in London by August, working in a Cold Storage Depot in Southwark but loses job after a fortnight. Returns to Longford and farm work. Obtains a post playing the piano in a cinema at Bude in December, but is retained for only a week

1922 Living in Plumstead, London, in January, working as a cinema pianist. Returns to his aunt's house in Longford in the following month and takes up farm work again. Dorothy, his younger sister, types out his poems for him and in May he submits third collection, *80 Poems*, to Sidgwick & Jackson who reject them. Loses third farm job in a month. Essay on 'The Springs of Music' published in *Musical Quarterly* in July. Begins work at Gloucester Tax Office, but loses job after twelve weeks. Moves in uninvited with his younger brother, Ronald, in Gloucester. Makes several suicide attempts. Certified insane on 28 September and admitted to Barnwood House, a private asylum near Gloucester. Makes two unsuccessful escape attempts. Moved to the City of London Mental Hospital at Dartford, known as Stone House, 21 December

1923 Escapes, 6 January, and travels to London to visit J. C. Squire and Vaughan Williams. Recaptured two days

later. Mental condition treated with Malarial injections in
August, to little effect. Publications include poems in the
Spectator and the *London Mercury*, piano music and a
song cycle, *Ludlow and Teme*

1924   Mental condition deteriorates in March. Sends out appeals
in August, listing seven collections of poetry that he
wishes to have typed, only one of which – *Rewards of
Wonder* – is now identifiable. Squire publishes poems in
his anthology, *Second Selections from Modern Poets* and the
London Mercury. Gurney correcting typescripts of poems
and writing new poetry and music by December

1925   Prolific output of songs and poems between January and
June, including nine volumes of poetry. Treated between
March and May by Dr Randolph Davis, with whom he
forms a rapport. Condition improves slightly in July and
Marion Scott and Vaughan Williams make plans to
transfer Gurney to Dr Davis's care as a private patient.
These are abandoned suddenly in December

1926   Dr Hart, a Harley Street psychiatrist, consulted about
Gurney's condition in January. Writes a play called *The
Tewkesbury Trial* in April. The song cycle, *The Western
Playland (and of sorrow)*, published the same month.
Prolific output of poetry between June and November but
turns to prose when mental condition deteriorates.
Severely deluded by December, believing himself to be
Shakespeare, Hilaire Belloc, Beethoven and Haydn,
amongst others

1927   Treated by Mr Lidderdale, a Christian Science practitioner,
between February and April. Revises and 'corrects' Walt
Whitman's poems in May. Deteriorates physically and
becomes hostile to staff and fellow-patients in June

1928   OUP publish five songs. Gollancz express interest in a
collection of his poems

1932   Visited by Helen Thomas, widow of Edward Thomas.

1935   Plans are made for the publication of a symposium on
Gurney's life and work in *Music and Letters*

1937   Becomes 'much weaker' physically and mentally in July.
Diagnosed as suffering from pleurisy and tuberculosis in
November. Dies from bilateral pulmonary tuberculosis,

26 December, and is buried on New Year's Eve at Twigworth,
Gloucestershire

1938　　Symposium on his work appears in *Music and Letters* in
January. OUP publish two volumes of his songs

Introduction

Walter de la Mare, contributing to the symposium on Ivor Gurney's life and work in *Music and Letters* in 1938, lamented the fact that Gurney's name was still 'unfamiliar, if not unknown' to 'lovers of English poetry'. The aim of the symposium, which included essays by Ralph Vaughan Williams, Edmund Blunden, J. C. Squire and Herbert Howells, was to provoke a re-evaluation of his work, but for Gurney himself this attempt at rehabilitation came too late. Shown the proofs on his deathbed, he was too weak to undo the wrappings. Thus what was intended as a celebration became a valediction. It was Squire, who had done much to make Gurney's poetry known in the pages of the *London Mercury*, who provided the most accurate assessment of the situation, writing ruefully: 'It will all come out some day, I suppose. But the best in the arts still has the old struggle.'

The struggle to achieve due recognition for Gurney's poetry carried on for the next forty years. His poems were never completely forgotten and were frequently anthologised, attracting such notable supporters as W. H. Auden, Geoffrey Grigson and Philip Larkin. But attempts to make more texts available met with little success. Edmund Blunden produced an edition of uncollected poems in 1954, but it was received with indifference. A later selection, edited by Leonard Clark and including material from the two books Gurney published in his lifetime, *Severn & Somme* (1917) and *War's Embers* (1919), appeared in 1973 to a similarly disappointing response. It was not until the publication of Michael Hurd's *The Ordeal of Ivor Gurney* in 1978 that the tide began to turn. This authoritative biography stressed the quality of Gurney's verse and provided copious examples of as yet unpublished poems and letters. The consensus amongst reviewers was that a new edition of the poetry was needed and this came in 1982 with P. J. Kavanagh's *Collected Poems of Ivor Gurney*, which showed at last the full range of Gurney's achievement and paved the way for a reprint of *Severn & Somme* and *War's Embers* and further editions of his poems and letters. This current selection, placing him in a series of important English poets, is intended to confirm that recognition.

There are a number of reasons – some biographical, some literary – why it took so long for Gurney's poetry to be appreciated. First, as the *Music and Letters* symposium stressed, he was a composer as well as a poet and, at the time of his death, his published verse amounted to two small books and a handful of poems in newspapers and journals. Far more of his music had been performed and published and, even when they appeared, Blunden's and Clark's editions were relatively modest in scope. This meant that not only was comparatively little of Gurney's poetry available but also that he was better known and respected as a composer, implying that his poetry was merely a hobby and not to be taken as seriously as the subject he had studied. This impression is reinforced by the poetry itself; the directness and apparent artlessness of his work, especially the later poems, seems to imply that he did not value his writing as much as his music.

Second, there is the question of Gurney's madness. He suffered from mental illness for most of his adult life and spent his last fifteen years in the asylum. This fact prejudiced responses to his work – if Gurney was a hobby poet, then he was also a 'mad poet' and the cases of Christopher Smart and John Clare show how difficult it is for poets so labelled to be accepted. It also meant that when Gurney did change and develop his style away from more conventional modes of writing, his innovations could be ascribed not to conscious artistry but to his condition. His earliest poems could be categorised as Georgian, but when he developed a new, idiosyncratic mode of expression – fortified by his beloved Elizabethan writers and Walt Whitman – he became neither a Georgian nor a Modernist. There are traces of both styles in his work. Rather than accept that he might have been doing something new, it was easier for critics to consider his innovations the effect of insanity and thus ignore them.

Labelling Gurney as simply a mad poet is a temptation but it fails to appreciate the precise qualities of his writing. So many of his asylum poems read like fragments of an uncompleted autobiography and indeed it is the intimacy, directness and cathartic qualities of poems like 'There is a man' or 'December 30th' that make them such powerful utterances. Yet once it is recognised that his style in these poems is a development of his earlier techniques, they can be reassessed in a proper light. His queer contractions, bizarre punctuation and confusing ellipses give the impression that he is no longer in control of either language or form but, based on the evidence of his earlier work, it is obvious that these are conscious stylistic techniques. He may have been 'In Hell . . . buried a score-depth, writing verse pages' ('Hell's Prayer') but he was nevertheless producing controlled artistic creations.

A third reason why Gurney's poetry was not recognised is that it resists easy categorisation. Take for example the inclusion of his name on the monument to the poets of the Great War, unveiled in Westminster Abbey in 1985. His wartime experiences are a recurrent theme in his verse and he has been a staple of anthologies of war poetry since 'To the Poet before Battle' was included in E. B. Osborn's *The Muse in Arms* in 1917; he also took to calling himself 'First war poet' in his asylum writings. Yet his war poems are quite unlike those of his more famous contemporaries, Wilfred Owen and Siegfried Sassoon. Whilst he shares with them an awareness of the hardships and suffering that war brings ('Pain', 'Strange Hells') and a dislike of civilian wartime rhetoric ('To the Prussians of England') he is concerned not so much with protest as with capturing ordinary individual experience – usually his own.

He points out in the Preface to *Severn & Somme* that 'Most of the book is concerned with a person named Myself', and he focuses on what might best be described as the domestic aspects of the Western Front: the importance of rations ('Laventie'), finding a good billet ('La Gorgues'), the companionship of service life ('Farewell'). He also celebrates the unexpected in wartime – for example the 'loathing and fine beauty' of the landscape in 'Near Vermand' or the pragmatic anti-heroism of the non-commissioned ('The Silent One', 'Of Grancourt') and he writes of these things not from a universal viewpoint that seeks to make sense of them, but from a subjective, intimate position. Like Whitman, he sings of himself; again, like Whitman, he is democratic and celebrates the common man, in this case the ordinary private.

It is typical of Gurney that he can find natural beauty to praise even in the landscape of war-torn France. The natural world – especially the beauties of his native Gloucestershire – are a central theme of his work, but again the subjectivity inherent in his treatment of it makes it difficult to describe him solely as a 'nature poet' or a 'local poet'. He may allude to his favourite places –

Crickley, Brimscombe, the Malverns – but these are merely the focus for his own personal perceptions and responses. Ultimately his poems have less to do with their ostensible subjects than with his own awareness of them as spiritual revelations. His is a real Gloucestershire, but it is a Gloucestershire reshaped in his imagination, and the reader needs no knowledge of its topography or its geographical reality to understand that it is for him a spiritual paradise.

His subjectivity also means that he avoids the vague generalisations and idealisations of many of his contemporaries when writing in a pastoral vein. Gurney's natural world is real, closely observed, and carefully recorded – again and again, in poems like 'Moments' and 'The Miracles', he shows his awareness of the transience of what he sees and the need to record it. He recreates what he sees so as to make it fresh again; 'Casual and common is the wonder grown', he says in 'Longford Dawns' and his celebration of the incense bearers in the poem of the same name or his visualisation of the banks of the river Severn as a theatrical space ('By Severn') are attempts to revitalise this wonder. Skies and the seasons are his favourite inspirations in this respect and their changing moods frequently find their way into his poems – playful stars at night ('Stars Sliding'), for example, or smudgy dawns 'scarfed in military colours' and 'wine scarlet' autumnal woods ('Old thought').

Another reason why Gurney fits uneasily into the category of nature poet is his fascination with the urban and man-made. Cities like Gloucester and London have their value, as do the marks of civilisation upon the pastoral landscape – farms, churches, 'great stone cisterns' and 'worthy mounting stones' ('Encounters'). As with his treatment of the rural world, he is concerned to preserve the transient and threatened, as in poems like 'Time to Come', which laments the development of new housing in Gloucester and how it affects the shape of the city. His perception of the landscape, both urban and rural, is coloured by historical survival, and history is for Gurney a human experience: the ploughing up of a Roman coin makes him think not of empires or dynasties but of 'some hurt centurion' who lived in the land of the past. His landscapes are peopled by such figures, some famous – London is the home of his Elizabethan 'masters' – and some obscure, like the anonymous kiln-makers and church builders of Gloucestershire. All contribute to his imaginative geography.

His fascination with people – his democracy – also means that he avoids the consciously poetic subject and celebrates instead the mundane and commonplace. Kilns are as important as cathedrals for him and cabbages as worthy of celebration in verse as 'that ink-proud lady the rose' ('The Garden'). Tobacco, too, deserves acknowledgement as 'the king of comfort bringers' and even something as ordinary as a kettle boiling or washing hanging out to dry can become, for Gurney, both the occasion of a poem and yet remain its own intrinsic self, 'It's own for ever; alive, dead, my possession' ('The Miracles').

This edition gives Gurney's texts exactly as he – or, in the case of poems that only survive in typescript, his typists – wrote them down. This gives an accurate picture of his development and, although it may produce strange-looking poems, they are never incomprehensible and it becomes clear how important Gurney's punctuation is as an element of his style. It is not only his new coinages such as 'novembery' or 'toadiness' or his delight in colloquialisms that make Gurney's poems so individual and innovative: it is the way in which he captures the flow of his imagination in the novelties of his grammar and punctuation.

The poems are arranged to show the development of Gurney's creativity whilst at the same time illustrating the breadth of his style and subject matter, from his shorter intimate lyrical pieces to his more challenging discursive meditations on writers, war, history, the landscape and his own experiences. The order is, as far as is possible, chronological – from 'To the Poet before Battle', his first published poem written in August 1915, to 'The Wind', seemingly his last poem, written in March 1929. The reader can thus see how Gurney moves from the Georgian conventionality of his earliest poems into a period of deliberate experimentation between 1920 and 1922, through the individuality of his first three and a half years in the asylum and finally into the simplicity and completeness of the later asylum poems.

At the end of his creative life, Gurney was able to write in 'The Wind': 'My days were amply long, and I content / In their achievement'. This edition serves as an introduction to the best of that achievement.

GEORGE WALTER

Ivor Gurney

I. July 1915–1919

To the Poet before Battle

Now, youth, the hour of thy dread passion comes:
Thy lovely things must all be laid away;
And thou, as others, must face the riven day
Unstirred by rattle of the rolling drums,
Or bugles' strident cry. When mere noise numbs   5
The sense of being, the fear-sick soul doth sway,
Remember thy great craft's honour, that they may say
Nothing in shame of poets. Then the crumbs
Of praise the little versemen joyed to take
Shall be forgotten: then they must know we are,   10
For all our skill in words, equal in might
And strong of mettle as those we honoured; make
The name of poet terrible in just war,
And like a crown of honour upon the fight.

Strange Service

Little did I dream, England, that you bore me
Under the Cotswold hills beside the water meadows,
To do you dreadful service, here, beyond your borders
And your enfolding seas.

I was a dreamer ever, and bound to your dear service,   5
Meditating deep, I thought on your secret beauty,
As through a child's face one may see the clear spirit
Miraculously shining.

Your hills not only hills, but friends of mine and kindly,
Your tiny knolls and orchards hidden beside the river   10
Muddy and strongly-flowing, with shy and tiny streamlets
Safe in its bosom.

Now these are memories only, and your skies and rushy
    sky-pools
Fragile mirrors easily broken by moving airs . . .
In my deep heart for ever goes on your daily being,   15
And uses consecrate.

Think on me too, O Mother, who wrest my soul to serve
    you
In strange and fearful ways beyond your encircling waters;
None but you can know my heart, its tears and sacrifice;
None, but you, repay.   20

Bach and the Sentry

Watching the dark my spirit rose in flood
   On that most dearest Prelude of my delight.
The low-lying mist lifted its hood,
   The October stars showed nobly in clear night.

When I return, and to real music-making,   5
   And play that Prelude, how will it happen then?
Shall I feel as I felt, a sentry hardly waking,
   With a dull sense of No Man's Land again?

Song

Only the wanderer
　　Knows England's graces,
Or can anew see clear
　　Familiar faces.

And who loves joy as he　　　　　　　　5
　　That dwells in shadows?
Do not forget me quite,
　　O Severn meadows.

Pain

Pain, pain continual; pain unending;
Hard even to the roughest, but to those
Hungry for beauty . . . Not the wisest knows,
Nor most pitiful-hearted, what the wending
Of one hour's way meant. Grey monotony lending　　5
Weight to the grey skies, grey mud where goes
An army of grey bedrenched scarecrows in rows
Careless at last of cruellest Fate-sending.
Seeing the pitiful eyes of men foredone,
Or horses shot, too tired merely to stir,　　　　　　10
Dying in shell-holes both, slain by the mud.
Men broken, shrieking even to hear a gun. –
Till pain grinds down, or lethargy numbs her,
The amazed heart cries angrily out on God.

Ballad of the Three Spectres

As I went up by Ovillers
  In mud and water cold to the knee,
There went three jeering, fleeing spectres,
  That walked abreast and talked of me.

The first said, 'Here's a right brave soldier   5
  That walks the dark unfearingly;
Soon he'll come back on a fine stretcher,
  And laughing for a nice Blighty.'

The second, 'Read his face, old comrade,
  No kind of lucky chance I see;   10
One day he'll freeze in mud to the marrow,
  Then look his last on Picardie.'

Though bitter the word of these first twain
  Curses the third spat venomously;
'He'll stay untouched till the war's last dawning   15
  Then live one hour of agony.'

Liars the first two were. Behold me
  At sloping arms by one – two – three;
Waiting the time I shall discover
  Whether the third spake verity.   20

To the Prussians of England

When I remember plain heroic strength
And shining virtue shown by Ypres pools,
Then read the blither written by knaves for fools
In praise of English soldiers lying at length,
Who purely dream what England shall be made   5
Gloriously new, free of the old stains
By us, who pay the price that must be paid,
Will freeze all winter over Ypres plains.
Our silly dreams of peace you put aside
And Brotherhood of man, for you will see   10
An armed Mistress, braggart of the tide
Her children slaves, under your mastery.
We'll have a word there too, and forge a knife,
Will cut the cancer threatens England's life.

'My heart makes songs on lonely roads'

My heart makes songs on lonely roads
To comfort me while you're away,
And strives with lovely sounding words
Its crowded tenderness to say.

Glimmering against the forward dark,   5
Your face I see with pride, with pain
So that one time I did desire
Never to see that face again.

But I am glad that Love has come
To bind me fast and try my worth;   10
For Love's a powerful Lord and gives
His friends dominion over the earth.

Photographs

(To Two Scots Lads)

Lying in dug-outs, joking idly, wearily;
   Watching the candle guttering in the draught;
Hearing the great shells go high over us, eerily
   Singing; how often have I turned over, and laughed

With pity and pride, photographs of all colours,   5
   All sizes, subjects: khaki brothers in France;
Or mother's faces worn with countless dolours;
   Or girls whose eyes were challenging and must dance,

Though in a picture only, a common cheap
   Ill-taken card; and children – frozen, some   10
(Babies) waiting on Dicky-bird to peep
   Out of the handkerchief that is his home

(But he's so shy!). And some with bright looks, calling
   Delight across the miles of land and sea,
That not the dread of barrage suddenly falling   15
   Could quite blot out – not mud nor lethargy.

Smiles and triumphant careless laughter. O
   The pain of them, wide Earth's most sacred things!
Lying in dugouts, hearing the great shells slow
   Sailing mile-high, the heart mounts higher and sings.   20

But once – O why did he keep that bitter token
   Of a dead Love? – that boy, who, suddenly moved,
Showed me, his eyes wet, his low talk broken,
   A girl who better had not been beloved.

To his Love

He's gone, and all our plans
   Are useless indeed.
We'll walk no more on Cotswold
   Where the sheep feed
   Quietly and take no heed.   5

His body that was so quick
   Is not as you
Knew it, on Severn river
   Under the blue
   Driving our small boat through.   10

You would not know him now . . .
   But still he died
Nobly, so cover him over
   With violets of pride
   Purple from Severn side.   15

Cover him, cover him soon!
   And with thick-set
Masses of memoried flowers –
   Hide that red wet
   Thing I must somehow forget.   20

Above Ashleworth

O does some blind fool now stand on my hill
To see how Ashleworth nestles by the river?
Where eyes and heart and soul may drink their fill.

The Cotswolds range out Eastward as if never
A curve of them the hand of Time might change;   5
Beauty sleeps most confidently for ever.

The blind fool stands, his dull eyes free to range
Endlessly almost, and finds no word to say;
Not that the sense of wonder is too strange

Too great for speech. Naught touches him; the day   10
Blows its glad trumpets, breathes rich-odoured breath;
Glory after glory passes away.

(And I'm in France!). He looks, and sees beneath
The clouds in steady Severn silver and grey.
But dead he is, and comfortable in Death.   15

Turmut-hoeing

I straightened my back from turmut-hoeing
    And saw, with suddenly opened eyes,
Tall trees, a meadow ripe for mowing,
    And azure June's cloud-circled skies.

Below, the earth was beautiful   5
    Of touch and colour, fair each weed,
But Heaven's high beauty held me still,
    Only of music had I need.

And the white-clad girl at the old farm,
    Who smiled and looked across at me,   10
Dumb was held by that strong charm
    Of cloud-ships sailing a foamless sea.

Toussaints

(To J.W.H.)

Life softly clanging cymbals were
Plane-trees, poplars Autumn had
Arrayed in gloriously sad
Garments of beauty wind-astir;
It was the day of all the dead –   5

Toussaints. In sombre twos and threes
Between those coloured pillars went
Drab mourners. Full of presences
The air seemed . . . ever and anon rent
By a slow bell's solemnities.   10

The past year's gloriously dead
Came, folk dear to that rich earth
Had given them sustenance and birth,
Breath and dreams and daily bread,
Took labour-sweat, returned them mirth.   15

Merville across the plain gleamed white,
The thronged still air gave never a sound,
Only, monotonous untoned
The bell of grief and lost delight.
Gay leaves slow fluttered to the ground.   20

Sudden, that sense of peace and prayer
Like vapour faded. Round the bend
Swung lines of khaki without end . . .
Common was water, earth and air;
Death seemed a hard thing not to mend.   25

Equal Mistress

The tiny daisies are
Not anything
Less dear than the great star
Riding in the west afar
To their Mistress Spring.   5

Jupiter, the Pleiades
To her equal
With celandine and cress,
Stone-crop, freckled pagles
And birdseye small.   10

Since in her heart of love
No rank is there,
Nor degree aught, hers is
The most willing service
And free of care.   15

Violets, stars, birds
Wait on her smile, all
Too soon shall August come
Sheaves, fruit, be carried home,
And the leaves fall.   20

The Valley

There was such beauty in the dappled valley
As hurt the sight, the heart stabbed to tears.
The gathered beautifulness of all the years
Hovered thereover, it seemed, eternally
Set for men's joy. Town, tower, trees, river   5
Under a sky royal-azure Heaven for ever
Up-piled with towering mountains of March cloud.

A Herald-day of Spring more wonderful
Than Her true own. Trumpets cried aloud
In sky, earth, blood. No beast, no clod so dull   10
But the strength felt of the day, Power of the giver
Was glad for being, lowly at once, and proud.
Kyrie Eleison, and Gloria,
Credo, Jubilate, Magnificat:
The whole world gathered strength to praise the day.   15

The Companions

On uplands bleak and bare to wind
Beneath a maze of stars I strode;
Phantoms of Fear haunted the road,
Dogging my footsteps close behind.

Till Heaven blew clear of cloud, showed each   5
Most tiny baby-star as fine
As any jewel of kings. Orion
Triumphed through bare tracery of beech.

So unafraid I journeyed on
Past dusky rut and pool alight   10
With Heaven's chief wonder of night
Jupiter, close companion.

And in no mood of pride, courteous
Light-hearted, as with a king's friend,
He went with me to the journey's end   15
His courtiers Mars and Regulus.

My door reached, gladly had I paid
With stammered thanks his courtesy
And theirs, but ne'er a star could see
Of all Heaven's ordered cavalcade.   20
The inky pools naught held but shade,
Fine snow drove West and blinded me.

'When from the curve of the wood's edge'

When from the curve of the wood's edge does grow
Power, and that spreads to envelope me –
Wrapped up in sense of meeting tree and plough
I feel tiny song stir tremblingly,
And deep; the many birth-pangs separate   5
Taking most full of Joy, for soon shall come
The kindling, the beating at Heaven gate
The flood of tide that bears strongly home.

Then under the skies I make my vows
Myself to purify and fit my heart   10
For the inhabiting of the high House
Of Song, that dwells high and clean apart
The fire, the flood, the soaring, these the three
That merged are power of Song and prophecy.

II. 1920–September 1922

Western Sky-Look

When clouds shake out their sails
Before delighted gales,
I think the sailor-men at sea,
Hearing the engine throbbing free
Curse their today's fate that they must   5
Defeat Magellan with black dust,
Scrape deck plates till the nerves are worn – ;
Whose fathers froze in desperate weather
Sail-handling in Death's despite together.
Here's never work that's fit for man,   10
Bristol Cabot, Drake, Magellan
Set man's strength square against the sea,
With courage broken and bulwarks lashed,
And seventh-Hell battle never drawn;
While here and now pale Duty does   15
Domestic service on bright brass. . . .
The sailor-men lift heart and eyes
To the thronged skies:
They cleave the air, leap winged to shake
More sails, more sails out; watch the wake   20
Of cirrus lengthen on the blue,
And run clean sailor-work to do . . .
Fall sheer . . . to waste and paraffin –
Pistons gone tired of out-and-in,
Hard work as black and dull as sin.   25

The Change

Gone bare the fields now, and the starlings gather,
Whirr above stubble and soft changing hedges.
Changed the season chord too, F major or minor,
The gnats sing thin in clouds above the sedges.

And there is nothing proud now, nor disconsolate   5
Nothing youthful save where dark crocus flings
Summer's last challenge toward Winter's merciless
Cohort, for whom the robin alone sings.

Fields for a while longer, then, O soul,
A curtained room close shut against the rime –   10
Where shall float Music, voice or violins
Denial passionate of the frozen time

The Songs I had

The songs I had are withered
Or vanished clean,
Yet there are bright tracks
Where I have been,

And there grow flowers   5
For other's delight.
Think well, O singer,
Soon comes night.

London Dawn

Dawn comes up on London,
And night's undone.
Stars are routed
And street lamps outed.
Sodden great clouds begin sail again   5
Like all-night anchored galleons to the main
From careful shallows to the far-withdrawn
Wide outer seas of sky,
Sleepers above river change their pain,
Lockhart's shows lively up Blackfriars Lane   10
Motors dash by
With 'Mirrors', 'Mails', 'Telegraphs' what not?
South shore of Thames on London shows a blot,
And first careful coffee-stall is withdrawn.

Only the poet strolls about at ease,   15
Wondering what mortal thing his soul may please,
And spitting at the drains, while Paul's as ever
Is mighty and a king of sky and river,
And cares no more, Much-Father, for this one
Broke child, although a poet-born and clever,   20
Than any spit-kid of seven million,
Must drudge all daylight till his earnings done.
A huffler has her red sails just a quiver;
Sun's very near now and the tide's a-run.

Generations

The ploughed field and the fallow field
They sang a prudent song to me;
We bide all year and take our yield
Or barrenness as case may be.

 What time or tide may bring to pass   5
Is nothing of our reckoning,
Power was before our making was
That had in brooding thought it's spring.

We bide our fate as best betides
What ends the tale may prove the first.   10
Stars know as truly of their guides
As we the truth of best or worst.

Moments

I think the loathed minutes one by one
That tear and then go past are little worth
Save nearer to the blindness to the sun
They bring me, and the farewell to all earth

Save to that six-foot-length I must lie in   5
Sodden with mud, and not to grieve again
Because high Autumn goes beyond my pen
And snow lies inexprest in the deep lane.

When I am covered

When I am covered with the dust of peace
And but the rain to moist my senseless clay,
Will there be one regret left in that ill ease

One sentimental fib of light and day –
A grief for hillside and the beaten trees?   5
Better to leave them, utterly to go away.

When every tiny pang of love is counterpiece
To shadowed woe of huge weight and the stay
For yet another torment ere release

Better to lie and be forgotten aye.   10
In Death his rose-leaves never is a crease.
Rest squares reckonings Love set awry.

Longford Dawns

Of course not all the watchers of the dawn
See Severn mists like forced-march mists withdraw
London has darkness changing into light
With just one quarter hour of any weight.

Casual and common is the wonder grown, –   5
Time's duty to lift lights curtain up and down.
But here Time is caught up clear in Eternity
And draws as breathless life as you or me.

Saturday's comings

The horses of day plunge and are restrained
Dawn broadens to quarter height, and the meadow mists
Drift like gauze veilings, the roadway ingrained
With traffic marks shows so, Saturday enters the lists

To show like a panorama cattle brought in   5
And dapper farmers bargaining in white spats,
Cross crowded, bookstalls past paupers resisting
And as ever the Cathedral masterfully blessing the flats.

Had I a song

Had I a song
I would sing it here
Four lined square shaped
Utterance dear

But since I have none,   5
Well, regret in verse
Before the power's gone
Might be worse, might be worse.

What evil coil

What evil coil of Fate has fastened me
Who cannot move to sight, whose bread is sight,
And in nothing has more bare delight
Than dawn or the violet or the winter tree.
Stuck-in-the-mud – Blinkered-up, roped for the Fair   5
What use to vessel breath that lengthens pain?
O but the empty joys of wasted air
That blow on Crickley and whimper wanting me!

The hoe scrapes earth

The hoe scrapes earth as fine in grain as sand,
I like the swirl of it and the swing in the hand
Of the lithe hoe so clever at craft and grace,
And the friendliness the clear freedom of the place.

And the green hairs of the wheat on the sandy brown   5
The draw of eyes toward the coloured town,
The lark ascending slow to a roof of cloud
That cries for the voice of poetry to cry aloud

Defiance

I will not droop my soiléd flag,
Nor turn a thought on my own shame,
Though it be sin without a name,
And smutted honour but a rag
There is a curve of Glo'ster plough   5
That I was born alone to show.

If I go down before my fear
Has limned that shape with subtle truth
Mine ending be a thing of ruth
And best forgot by honest men.   10
Come then, night's near with much undone
And Time's fine sand too swift doth run.

Encounters

One comes across the strangest things in walks,
Fragment of Abbey tithe barns fixed in modern,
With Dutch-sort houses, where the water baulks
Weired up, and brick-kilns broken among fern.
Old troughs, great stone cisterns bishops might have blessed   5
And baptized from, most worthy mounting stones;
Black timber in red brick, surprisingly placed
Where hill stone was looked for, and a manor's bones
Spied in the frame of some wisteria'd house,
And mill-falls and sedge-pools, and Saxon faces   10

Stream sources happened upon in unlikely places
And Roman looking hills of small degree.
The surprise, the good in dignity of poplars
At a roads end, or the white Cotswold scars.
Sheets spread out spotless against the hazel tree.   15

But toothless old men, bubbling over with jokes
And deadly serious once the speaking finished.
Beauty is less after all than strange comical folks
And the wonder of them never and never can become diminished.

Lovely playthings

Dawn brings lovely playthings to the mind,
But sunset fights and goes down in battle blind.
The banners of dawn spread over in mystery,
But nightfall ends a boast and a pageantry.

After the halt of dawn comes the slow moving of   5
Time till the sun's hidden rush and the day is admitted.
Sunset dies out in a smother of something like love,
With dew and the elm-hung stars and owl outcries half-witted.

Rainy Midnight

Long shines the line of wet lamps dark in gleaming,
The trees so still felt yet as strength not used,
February chills April, the cattle are housed,
And nights grief from the higher things comes streaming.

The traffic is all gone, the elver-fishers gone   5
To string their lights 'long Severn like a wet Fair.

If it were fine the elvers would swim clear,
Clothes sodden, the out-of-work stay on.

Personages

Beauty and bright fame go not together, I
Bought oranges to-day from Queen Deirdre.
Apollo hewed the beech, I stood and watched
A ghost of wonder weaving while one thatched;
A pattern of lithe movements all a wonder: 5
An axe one farmer dealt like Zeus his thunder,
But no harm came save splinters on the dog.
Rosalind milks brown Jerseys Brimscombe way,
With careless royal air born of the first breath
And stealthy air-stirrings of breaking day.   10
Young gods a many hew stubborn at their log,
Strong labours show the breed plain underneath,
And goddesses a many near

April Gale

The wind frightens my dog, but I bathe in it,
Sound, rush, scent of the Spring fields.

My dog's hairs are blown like feathers askew,
My coat's a demon, torturing like life.

Common Things

The dearness of common things –
Beech wood, tea, plate-shelves,
And the whole family of crockery –
Wood-axes, blades, helves.

Ivory milk, earth's coffee,   5
The white face of books
And the touch, feel, smell of paper –
Latin's lovely looks.

Earth fine to handle;
The touch of clouds,   10
When the imagining arm leaps out to caress
Grey worsted or wool clouds.

Wool, rope, cloth, old pipes
Gone, warped in service;
And the one herb of tobacco,   15
The herb of grace, the censer weed,
Of whorled, blue, finger-traced curves.

The Road

Out beyond Aldgate is a road,
And a broad,
Clean, noble thing it runs,
For the sun's
And wind's and man's delight,   5
And the high stars at night.
There go Jewesses
And Poles and Russ and these
Pale-faced sons,
Daughter of Thames and Paul's   10

Betwixt walls and high walls
Of sooted brick, ugly turned.
A hard life, hardly earned;
Routine that galls,
Being so cunning turned.   15
Seldom marvellous
Comes down tremulous,
Or steady on that East
is light increased.
Through smoke-fog or river mist. . . .   20
Never fades the sun
Out in pageants that stun
The heart from talking thereon.
Always something mars
Magnificence from stars.   25
From strange faces and thunder
Men must draw wonder:
Thunder
Of trams and buses crammed,
Or Saturday-night damned-   30
Up, seething, dodging,
Grumbling, laughing, over-busy
Crowd in Mile End crammed;
Or in one hour of joys
When football plays   35
Marvellous music on these jigging heart-strings,
And one lucky kick brings
Battle-winning in a Niagara of noise –
Or some furtive
Trick of professionalism   40
Plunges a crowd into Hell's
Own tumult and scorn and hot-alive
Furious cataclysm –
The referee quells.
Or in sight of a painted   45
Face, through the tainted
Smoke-blue atmosphere
Of Music-hall, Cinema,
Where happy Tom Parker
Or Chaplin would grin him a   50

Further defiance of consequence here,
Or in drinkings of beer,
Or eatings of strange fish
Or shelled things from barrows;
Stewed eels, winkles: –   55
Roast pea-nut mingles
Well with the whole.
Or in sight of fallen horses
Or axle-broken wheeled things
The market-gardener brings   60
Or the hawker his cabbages,
Some Essex husbandryings
For London's vast maw.
Or fire-engine's law
Of free-way when the quickest sees   65
Smoke or sparks rising
In places surprising
And rings in fears' ecstasies.
For quick horseless carriages,
Brass-helmeted heroes –   70
But it might be advertising.
Anyhow folk live there
And daily strive there,
And earn their bread there,
Make friends, see red there,   75
As high on the clean hills
Where soft sea-rapture fills
The gladdened lungs.
And young souls are fleshed there
And tyrants immeshed there   80
As in Athens or Ukraine,
And the heart hurts the brain
Or the spirit is lashed there,
And thought is as vain,
Hope constant, and smashed there,   85
As away a day's journey by train.

The Square Thing

At Norton Green the tower stands well off road
And is a squareness meaning many things;
Nearest to us, the makers had abode
Beside the Northern road of priests and kings.

Men of a morning looked away to Wales 5
Or wavy Malvern under smoothy roof;
And said, that we have seen such hills and vales
Our churchkin here must give men certain proof.

And so from virtue mixed of sky and land
They raised a thing to match our equal dreams. 10
It was no common infire moved their hand,
Building so squarely among meadow streams.

Apprentices

We who praise poets with our labouring pen
And justify ourselves with laud of men
Have not the right to call our own our own,
Being but the ground-sprouts from those great trees grown.
The crafted art, the smooth curve, and surety 5
Come not of nature till the apprentice free
Of trouble with his tools, and cobwebbed cuts,
Spies out a path his own and casts his plots.
Then looking back on four-square edifices
And wind-and-weather standing tall houses 10
He stakes a court and tries his unpaid hand;
Begins a life who salt is arid sand;
Of cactus whose bread comes, whose wine is clear,
Being bitter water from fount all too near.
Happy if after toil he grow to worth 15
And prise of complete men of earlier birth

Of happier pen and more steel-propertied
Nerves of the capable and the mighty dead.

Time to Come

They will walk there, the sons of our great grandsons and
Will know no reason for the old love of the land.
There will be no tiny bent-browed houses in the
Twilight to watch, nor small shops of multi-miscellany.
The respectable and red-brick will rule all,   5
With green-paint railings outside the front door wall;
And children will not play skip-games in the gutter,
Nor dust fly furious in hot valour of footer;
Queerness and untidiness will be smoothed out
As with any steam-roller tactful, and there'll be no doubt   10
About the dust-bins or the colour of curtains,
No talking at the doors, no ten o'clock flirtings,
And Nicholas will look as strange as any
Goddess ungarmented in that staid company,
With lovely attitude of fixéd grace,   15
But naked and embarrassed in the red brick place.

We see her well, and should have great thanksgiving,
Living in sight and form of more than common living.
She is a City still and the centuries drape her yet;
Something in the air or light cannot or will not forget   20
The past ages of her, and the toil which made her,
The courage of her, the army that made not afraid her,
And a shapely fullness of being drawn maybe from the air;
Crystal or mellow about her or above her ever:
Record of desire, apparent of dreamer or striver;   25
And still the house between the Cotswolds bare
And the Welsh wars, Mistress of the widening river.

Generations

There are mummers yet on Cotswold,
Though Will Squele he lies low,
And men sow wheat on headlands
That other men see grow.

Eyes close and copper weights them;   5
Babes as blind come to birth;
Though John Gaunt's bets are ended
And shallow Shallow's mirth.

The Garden

The ordered curly and plain cabbages
Are all set out like school-children in rows;
In six short weeks shall these no longer please,
For with that ink-proud lady the rose, pleasure goes.

I cannot think what moved the poet men   5
So to write panegyrics of that foolish
Simpleton – while wild-rose as fresh again
Lives, and the drowsed cabbages keep soil coolish.

Daily

If one's heart is broken twenty times a day,
What easier thing than to fling the bits away,
But still one gathers fragments, and looks for wire,
Or patches it up like some old bicycle tire.

Bicycle tires fare hardly on roads, but the heart   5
Has an easier time than rubber, they sheathe a cart
With iron, so lumbering and slow my mind must be made,
To bother the heart and to teach things and learn it its trade.

Darkness has cheating swiftness

Darkness has cheating swiftness
When the eyes rove
Opens and shuts in long avenues
That thought cannot prove.

Darkness shuts in and closes,   5
There are three ghosts
Different in one clump of hedge roses
And a threat in posts.

Until one tops the road crest.
Turns, sees the city lie   10
Long stretched out in bright sparkles of gratefullest
Homecalling array.

The Soaking

The rain has come, and the earth must be very glad
Of its moisture, and the made roads, all dust clad;
It lets a veil down on the lucent dark,
And not of any bright ground thing shows its spark.

Tomorrow's gray morning will show cowparsley,   5
Hung all with shining drops, and the river will be
Duller because of the all soddenness of things,
Till the skylark breaks his reluctance, hangs shaking, and sings.

Tobacco

When tobacco came, When Raleigh did first bring in
The unfabled herb, the plant of peace, the king
Of comfort bringers, then indeed new hope
Came to the host of poets – with new scope
New range of power, since henceforth one might sit
Midnight-on and still further, while the war of wit   5
More kindly became and coloured till dawn came in;
Piercing shutter-chinks with pale daylight thin

Raleigh he knew, but could not the impossible
War of swift steel and hurtled bronze foretell
Nor the imaginary hurt on body's vessel,   10
Nor how tobacco then would steady disastered
Nerves courage by gray terror almost mastered.
Gloucester men half a day or more would hide
Five cigarettes and matches well inside
Their breasts, the one thing unsodden, while despair   15
Dripped incessantly without interest from the air
Or go supperless
The better next day's tobacco taste to bless.
Wonder at fogs, stars, posts till headaches came
Those chief of trouble-comforts still the same –   20
Watch Verey lights, sandbags, grasses, rifle-sights, mud
Crampt in uncouth postures men crouched or stood –
A Woodbine breakfast inspiriting the blood.

Or in those caves of dugouts, man taking lazily
Smoke in luxuriously, of Woodbines easily,   25
For one stroke forgiving Fate and its so mazily
Selftangled knots. Easing the strained back,
Somehow or other slipping unseen from the rack
Into tobacco scent, or savour or look,
The divine virtue of some contenting book   30
Multiplying or in sunniest quiet resting
Loll into restlessness or sleepy jesting.
Tobacco truly taken, neat, as a Thing.
Tobacco tasted exactly: in waves or ring

Noted; tobacco blown to the wind, or watched   35
Melt into ether's farthest smother unmatched.
Keen Sentries whiffing surreptitiously,
Sly Fatigue parties hidden from scrutiny
Last breath favours begged desperately.

Over all the breath of the airy vapour is known   40
Life's curtain rises on it and Deaths trembles down
Heroism has taken it for sufficient crown

When I think of the Ark slapping hopeless waters
Or Aeneas' sailors cursed with unclean hunger
Or Irus and his scorn, or the legions Germanicus   45
Met, and was nearly scotted by whose anger,
I know, I realise, and am driven to pity
By sun scorched eternal days of Babylon City
And any unsoothed restless greedy clamour
As hunger for Empire, any use of Wars hammer,   50
Tea and tobacco after decent labour
Would bring again England of pipe and tabor
Merry England again, after four centuries,
Of dawn-rising and late talking and go-as you please

Half dead

Half dead with sheer tiredness, wakened quick at night
With dysentry pangs, going blind among sleepers
And dazed into half-dark, illness had its spite.
Head cleared, eyes saw; horrible body-creepers
Stilled with the cold – the cold bringing me sane –   5
See there was Witcombe Steep as it were, but no beeches there.
Yet still clear flames of stars over the crest bare,
Mysterious glowing on the cloths of heaven,

Best turn in, fatigue party out at seven
Dark was the billet after that seeing rare.   10

Near Vermand

Lying flat on my belly shivering in clutch frost,
There was time to watch the stars, we had dug in;
Looking eastward over the low ridge; March scurried its blast,
At our senses, no use either dying or struggling.
Low woods to left, Cotswold spinnies if ever,   5
Showed through snow flurries and the clearer star weather.
And nothing but chill and wonder lived in mind; nothing
But loathing and fine beauty, and wet clothing.
Here were thoughts. Cold smothering, and fire-desiring,
A day to follow like this or in digging or wiring.   10

Drachms + Scruples

Misery weighed by drachms and scruples
Is but scrawls on a vain page,
To cruel masters we are pupils,
Escape comes careless with old Age.

O why were stars so set in Heaven   5
To desire greedily as gluttons do;
Or children trinkets – May death make even
So rough an evil as we go through.

Stars Sliding

The stars are sliding wanton through trees,
The sky is sliding steady over all.
Great Bear to Gemini will lose his place
And Cygnus over world's brink slip + fall.

Follow-my-Leader's not so bad a game.   5
But were it leap frog: O to see the shoots
And tracks of glory; Scorpions and Swans tame
And Argo swarmed with Bulls and other brutes.

Brown earth Look

The youth burning couch grass is as tired
As muscle has right to bear and keeps work on
The brown earth slopes from the potato field to the wired
Sheep enclosure; and hidden high and white the sun.

Brown the sense of things, the light smoke blows across   5
The field face, light blue wisps of sweet bitter reek
Dear to the Roman perhaps, so old seems the dross
Burning of root, grass, wheat, so near, easy to seek.

Old is the land a thousand generations
Have tilled there, sought with bright sweat the stuff of its
    bread   10
Here one comes for the sense of fine books, revelations
Of beauty in usualty, found as well of heart as of head.

And all the tales of far Europe that come on one,
The sense of myriads tending the needings of life
And more to one than the near memory of battle gun   15
Peace with its sorrow blots out the agonie's of strife.

When March blows

When March blows, and Monday's linen is shown
On the goose berry bushes, and the worried washer alone
Fights at the soaked stuff, meres and the rutted pools
Mirror the wool-pack clouds, and shine clearer than jewels

And the children throw stones in them, spoil mirrors and
    clouds   5
The worry of washing over; the worry of foods,
Brings tea-time; March quietens as the trouble dies.
The washing is brought in under wind-swept clear skies.

The Miracles

What things I have missed today, I know very well
But the seeing of them each new time is miracle,
Nothing between Bredon and Dursley has
Anyday yesterday's precise unpraiséd grace.
The changed light, or curve changed mistily   5
Coppice now bold cut: yesterday's mystery.
A sense of mornings, once seen, for ever gone,
It's own for ever; alive, dead, my possession

Robecq again

Robecq had straw and a comfortable tavern
There men might their sinews feel slowly recovering
From the march-strain and there was Autumn's translucence
in The calm air, and a tang of the earth and its essence.
A girl served wine there with natural dignity   5

Moving as any princess from care free,
And the North French air bathed crystal the flat land
With cabbages and tobacco plants and varied culture spanned.
Beautiful with moist clarity of Autumn's breath.
Lovely with the years turning to leafless death   10
Robecq, the dark town at night with estaminets lit,
The outside road with poplars, plane trees on it,
Huge dark barn with candles throwing warning flares
Glooms steady + shifting pierced with cold flowing airs,
With dumb peace at last and a wrapping from cares.   15

Kettle-song

The worry and low murmur
Of the black kettle are set
Against my unquiet achings
And vanish, so strong is the fret.

Such tangles and evil-skeined fibres   5
Of living so matted are grown
That water-song is hardly noticed
For all its past comfortings known.

Larches

Larches are most fitting small red hills
That rise like swollen antheaps likeably
And modest before big things like near Malvern
Or Cotswold's farther early Italian
Blue arrangement; unassuming as the   5
Cowslips, celandines, buglewort and daisies
That trinket out the green swerves like a child's game.

O never so careless or lavish as here,
I thought, 'You beauty! I must rise soon one dawn time
And ride to see the first beam strike on you   10
Of gold or ruddy recognisance over
Crickley level or Bredon sloping down.
I must play tunes like Burns, or sing like David,
A saying out of what the hill leaves unexprest
The tale or song that lives in it, and is sole,   15
A round red thing, green upright things of flame
It is May, and the conceited cuckoo toots and whoos his name.

Mist on Meadows

Mist lies heavy on English meadows
As ever in Ypres, but the friendliness
Here is greater in full field and hedge shadow.
And there is less menace and no dreadfulness
As when the Verey lights went up to show the land stark   5
Dreadful green light baring the ruined trees
Stakes, pools, lostness better hidden dreadful in dark
And not ever reminding of these other fields
Where tall dock and clover is, and that sweet grass yields
For that poisoned; where the cattle hoof makes mark,   10
And the river drifts slowly along the leas.

Old thought

Autumn that name of creeper falling and tea-time loving,
Was once for me the thought of High Cotswold noon-air,
And the earth smell, turning brambles, and half-cirrus
    moving,
Mixed with the love of body and travel of good turf there.

O up in height, O snatcht up O swiftly going,   5
Common to beechwood, breathing was loving, the yet
Unknown Crickley cliffs trumpeted, set music on glowing
In my mind. White Cotswold, wine scarlet woods and leaf
    wreckage wet.

Hedges

Bread and cheese grow wild in the green time,
Children laugh and pick it, and I make my rhyme
For mere pleasure of seeing that so subtle play,
Of arms and various legs going every any way.

And they turn and laugh for the unexpensiveness   5
Of country grocery and are pleased no less
Than hedge sparrows. Lessons will be easier taken,
For this gypsy chaffering, the hedge plucked and shaken.

The High Hills have a bitterness

The high hills have a bitterness
Now they are not known
And memory is poor enough consolation
For the soul helpless gone.
Up in the air there beech tangles wildly in the wind   5
That I can imagine
But the speed, the swiftness, walking into clarity,
Like last years bryony are gone.

Leckhampton Chimney has fallen down

Leckhampton chimney has fallen down
The birds of Crickley have cried it, it is known in the town,
The cliffs have changed, what will come next to that line
Watcher of West England, now that landmark has fallen

Severn has changed course, it is known by Barrow.   5
Malvern may heave up in other lines by tomorrow.
But Maisemore Hill stable and rounded shall stay
Not all the good influences will pass away

Cleeve will front sunset, Birdlip shall have its road
Flung angled and noble on its breast broad.   10
Many things shall stay, but the stone Chimney
Leckhamptons mark has fallen, like a stick or a tree.

When the body might free

When the body might free, and there was use in walking,
In October time – crystal air-time and free words were talking.
In my mind with light tunes and bright streams ran free.
When the earth smelt leaves shone and air and cloud had glee.

Then there was salt in life but now none is known,   5
To me who cannot go either where the white is blown
Of the grass, or scarlet willow herb of past memory.
Nothing is sweet to thinking, nothing from life free

Up there

On Cotswold edge there is a field and that
Grows thick with corn and speedwell and the mat
Of thistles, of that tall kind: Rome lived there,
Some hurt centurion got his grant or tenure
Built farm with fowls and pigsties and wood-piles   5
Waited for service custom between whiles.
The farmer ploughs up coins in the wet earth-time.
He sees them on the topple of crests gleam.
Or run down furrow, and halts and does let lie
Like a small black island in brown immensity.   10
Red pottery easy discovered no searching needed
One wonders what farms were like, no searching needed
As now the single kite hovering still
By the coppice there level with the flat of the hill.

Midnight

There is no sound within the cottage now,
But my pen and the sound of long rain
Heavy and musical, I must think again
To find so sweet a noise, and cannot anyhow.

The soothingness and deep-toned tinkle, soft   5
Happenings of night, in pain there's nothing better.
Save tobacco, or long most looked for letter. . . .
The different roof-sounds. House, shed, loft and scullery.

Sonnet. September 1922

Fierce indignation is best understood by those
Who have time or no fear, or a hope in its real good
One loses it with a filed soul or in sentimental mood
Anger is gone with sunset, or flows as flows
The water in easy mill-runs; the earth that ploughs   5
Forgets protestation in its turning, the rood
Prepares, considers, fulfils, and the poppy's blood
Makes old the old changing of the headlands brows.

But the toad under the harrow toadiness
Is known to forget, and even the butterfly   10
Has doubts of wisdom when that clanking thing goes by
And's not distressed. A twisted thing keeps still
That thing easier twisted than a grocers bill
And No history of November keeps the guy.

III. October 1922–December 1924

To God

Why have you made life so intolerable
And set me between four walls, where I am able
Not to escape meals without prayer, for that is possible
Only by annoying an attendant. And tonight a sensual
Hell has been put on me, so that all has deserted me   5
And I am merely crying and trembling in heart
For Death, and cannot get it. And gone out is part
Of sanity. And there is dreadful Hell within me.
And nothing helps. forced meals there have been and electricity
And weakening of sanity by influence   10
Thats dreadful to endure, and there is orders
And I am praying for death, death, death
And dreadful is the indrawing or out-breathing of breath
Because of the intolerable insults put on my whole soul
Of the soul loathed, loathed, loathed of the soul.   15
Gone out every bright thing from my mind.
All lost that ever God himself designed.
Not half can be written of cruelty of man, on man,
Not often such evil guessed as between Man and Man.

There is a man

There is a man who has swept or rubbed a floor
This morning crying in the Most Holy Name
Of God for Pity, and has not been able to claim
A moments respite, that for one hour, or more.
But can the not-conceiving heart outside   5
Believe the atmosphere that hangs so heavy

And clouds the torment, afterwards in the leavy
And fresher air, other torments may abide,
Or pass; and new pain, but this memory
Will not pass, it is too bad and the grinding   10
Remains, and what is better is the finding
Of any ease from working or changing free
Words between words, and cadences in change
But the pain is in thought, which will not freely range.

The Incense Bearers

To the London Metropolitan Police

Toward the sun the drenched May-hedges lift
White rounded masses like still ocean drift,
And days fills with heavy scent of that gift.

There is no escaping that full current of thick
Incense; one walks suddenly, one comes quick   5
Into a flood of odour there, aromatic

Not English, for cleaner, sweeter, is the hot scent that
Is given from hedges, solitary flowers, not
In mass, but lonely odours that scarcely float.

But the incense bearers, soakers of sun's full   10
Powerfulness; give out floods unchecked, wonderful
Utterance almost, which makes no poet grateful,

Since his love is for single things rarely found,
Or hardly. Violets blooming in remote ground.
One colour, one fragrance, like one uncompanied sound –   15

Struck upon silence, nothing looked for, hung
As from gold wires: this May incense is swung
Heavy of odour the drenched meadows among.

A wish

I would hope for the children of West Ham
Wooden-frame houses, square with some-sort stuff
Crammed in to keep the wind away that's rough,
And rain, in summer cool, in cold comfortable enough.
Easily destroyed – and pretty enough, and yet tough   5
Instead of brick and mortar tiled houses of no
Special appearance or attractive show.
Not crowded together, but with a plot of land
Where one might play and dig, and use spade or the hand
In managing or shaping earth in such forms,   10
As please the sunny mind or keep out of harms
The mind that's always good when let go its way
(I think) so there's work enough in a happy day.

Not brick and tile, but wood, thatch, walls of mixed
Material, and buildings in plain strength fixed.   15
Likeable, good to live in, easily pulled
Down, and in winter with warm ruddy light filled –
In summer with cool air; O better this sort of shelter –
And villages on the land set helter-skelter
On hillsides, dotted on plains; that the too exact   20
Straight streets of modern times that strait and strict
And formal keep man's spirit within bounds,
Where too dull duties keep in monotonous rounds

These villages to make for these towns of today –
O Haste – and England shall be happy with the May   25
Or meadow-reach to watch, miles to see and away.

I B Gurney
Stone House, Dartford, Kent (Appealing for Death
or Release.)

Old Times

Out in the morning
For a speed of thought I went
And a clear thought of scorning
For home keeping; while downward bent
Grass blades with dewdrops   5
Heavy on those delicate
Sword shapes, wonder thereat
Brightening my first hopes.

A four hours' tramping
With brisk blood flowing   10
And life worth knowing
For all that something
Which let happiness then
Sometimes not always
Breath-on-mirror of days   15
And all gone now, Since when?

On Somme

Suddenly into the still air burst thudding
And thudding and cold fear possessed me all,
On the gray slopes there, where Winter in sullen brooding
Hung between height and depth of the ugly fall
Of Heaven to earth; and the thudding was illness own.   5
But still a hope I kept that were we there going over
I; in the line, I should not fail, but take recover
From others courage, and not as coward be known.
No flame we saw, the noise and the dread alone
Was battle to us; men were enduring there such   10
And such things, in wire tangled, to shatters blown.

Courage kept, but ready to vanish at first touch.
Fear, but just held. Poets were luckier once
In the hot fray swallowed and some magnificence

The Escape

I believe in the increasing of life whatever
Leads to the seeing of small trifles . . . . . .
Real, beautiful, is good, and an act never
Is worthier than in freeing spirit that stifles
Under ingratitude's weight; nor is anything done   5
Wiselier than the moving or breaking to sight
Of a thing hidden under by custom; revealed
Fulfilled, used, (sound-fashioned) any way out to delight.
.   .   .   .
Trefoil . . . . hedge sparrow . . . the stars on the edge of night.   10

Thoughts of New England

Gloucester streets walking in Autumn twilight,
Past Kineburgh's cottage and old Raven Tavern,
That Hoare he kept, the Puritan, who tired
Or fired, and took a passage in the 'Mayflower',
Gloucester streets walking in frost-clear hour –   5
Of 'Captains Courageous' as a boy read, thinking,
And sea-ports, ships, and all that boy desired . . .
Walt Whitman, history-scraps and Huck Finn's cavern:
My thoughts went wondering how the New England Folk
Walked twilight now, watched stars steady or blinking –   10
If thoughts came Eastward as mine Westward went.
Of our 'Citizen', the 'Massachusetts Times',
And the boys crying them perhaps about their lanes.
But those no historied ground of Roman or Danes.

What are the streets that have no memories, 15
That are not underset by ancient rubbish?
Where gables overhang, and the quarters clang
From Cathedral towers, and the slops or dinner dish,
Hurried a man voids handily into the gutter:
And ghosts haunt the streets and of old troubles mutter. 20
Where steel and scarlet of the military
And routine use flash vivid momentarily;
Imagination stricken unaccountably
At full day into pictures not looked for even,
And children from their play by curfew driven. 25

Are there men of my blood over Atlantic
Wondering there what light is growing thick
By Severn and what real thing Cotswold is?
Are there men walking slow till tiredness leads in
To write or read till the night's veil grows thin; 30
Insatiate desiring what hope would win?
Is the air clear there as Thoreau's prose,
With frost and sparkling water, and day's close
As mild, as soft as shows in 'Evangeline'?
(Since all verse from the air or earth does win). 35

Do they hear tell of Domesday Book, and not
Think of this Gloucester where the scrivener wrote
Command of reeves first set their lists to begin?
Do they wish walk at evening where the earls went in
And William: Are there not crowns of England old 40
That first in Gloucester's Abbey showed their gold?
Can villas contain man in unloving hold
As here the cornered, the nooked low-ceilinged beetle-browed
Houses cloak man in; or the strict thoroughfares
Stone or asphalt-paved ally to man? 45

Are there great joys in April her high days
For those who cannot high imaginations see
Of other men builded, stirred to a great praise?
Cotswold earthing profound for white material,

Masses of stone gone slender as a silver birch,   50
Upwards in dazzle to an arching azure.

O where in the new towns shall recompense come,
For the market-days, the week-end trouble without measure,
The crowded four ways and cattle markets boom,
And country faces seen often with so much pleasure?   55

Can New England think deep thoughts of her bye-ways,
Is Abana and Pharpar a balance for
Severn receiving Avon, at her knot of highways,
Her Abbey township, beneath so high a cloud floor?

But nevertheless one would go very willingly   60
At the year's turn, where Washington or Lincoln walked,
Or praise 'Drum Taps' or 'This Compost', and hear talked
Speech of Lowell, or Hawthorne, or Holmes and be
Pleased with citizenship of Gloucester or Worcester
And companionship of veterans or veteran's sons   65
Of the Wilderness or Richmond, see the old guns
That set Chattanooga's thronged woods astir;
Or woke terror in steadfastness with red anger.

But not for longer than the strangeness lasted.
Severn yet calls not to be resisted: 70
And the mix of Dane thoughts, Roman, with Middle-Age
Calls all love out to mark on any page.

The glory of Peter's Abbey high up in Summer,
Or low in Winter's gloom, and a wavering shape,
Are more than is ever seen by foreign comer   75
To Connecticut, or Staten or Providence with its cape,
Being loveliness and history and height in one.

And there is nothing uprooted that is not changed.
Better to stay and wonder in the half light
How New England saunters where Kipling loved and ranged,   80
And watch the starling flocks in first autumn flight.

The New World has qualities its own,
But the Old not yet decrepit or withered is grown,

And brick and timber of age five centuries known
Are consolation for poverty enough   85
Against New York, where they say Opera is brilliant,
And the byeways with five dollar notes are strown.
The stuff of Liberty is a varying stuff,
But from Grant's men, Lee's men, nobleness should never want.

New Year's Eve

Aveluy and New Year's eve, and the time as tender
As if green buds grew. In the low West a slender
Streak of last orange. Guns mostly deadest still.
And a noise of limbers near, coming down the hill.
Nothing doing, nothing doing, and a screed to write,   5
Candles enough for books, a sleepy delight
In the warm dugout, day ended. Nine hours to the light.
There now and then now, one nestled down snug,
A head is enough to read by, and cover up with a rug.

Electric. Clarinet sang of a Hundred Pipers   10
(And hush-awe mystery vanishes like tapers
Of tobacco smoke,) there was a great hilarity then!
Breath and a queer tube magicked sorrow from men.
Here was no soul's cheat, friends were of love over there –
How past thought, returning sweet! yet the soldier must dare.   15

Smudgy Dawn

Smudgy dawn scarfed in military colours
Northward, and flowing wider like slow sea water,
Woke in lilac and elm and almost among garden flowers.
Birds a multitude; increasing as it made lighter.

Nothing but I moved by railings there; slept sweeter 5
Than kings the country folk in thatch or slate shade,
Peace had the grey West, fleece clouds sure in its power,
Out on much-Severn I thought waves readied for laughter
And the fire-swinger promised behind elm pillars
A day worthy such beginning to come after. 10

Brimscombe

One lucky hour in middle of my tiredness
I came under the pines of the sheer steep
And saw the stars like steady candles gleam
Above and through; Brimscombe wrapped (past life) in sleep!
Such body weariness and ugliness 5
Had gone before, such tiredness to come on me –
This perfect moment had such pure clemency
That it my memory has all coloured since,
Forgetting the blackness and pain so driven hence.
And the naked uplands even from bramble free. 10
That ringed-in hour of pines, stars, and dark eminence.
(The thing we looked for in our fear of France).

Cut Flowers

Not in blue vases these
Nor white, cut flowers are seen
But in the August meadows
When the reaper falls clean –
And the shining and ridged rows 5
Of cut stalks show to the eye
As if some child's hand there

Had ranged them, and passed by
To other rows, other swathes,
Moondaisies, pimpernel,   10
Eyebright, sorrel, the paths
Are shining, the heaps as well.
Violets in spring, are
In vases, a sweet heap
Better leave them by far   15
Under hedgerows or banks to keep.
Daffodills, wallflowers, Daisies
Of Michaelmas Time let still
Also, no gathering-crazes
Should spoil the sweet Spring-time's will   20
Daisies best left alone,
Chrysanthemums of chill
Evenings of Autumn, gone
Soon to cold Winters will.
At the full garden-folk   25
Leave in their beds, but if
Under the steely yoke
They must be gathered, With
Cruelty of no need.
Then lay them in wide pans,   30
Or open jars; agreed
Best pottery that is man's,
Wall-flowers, violets
Sweetest of flowers bring in
To the four walls, the china-sets   35
And table clean as a pin.
By books and pictures lay
These wild things cruelly tamed
Taken from the blowing day
Exiled, uprooted, hurt, lamed.   40
That the hedgerows miss and the copse –
O if flowers must be cut
To spoil an earth-plot's hopes.
Take them with eyes shut.
Or give a small coin or two   45
To Children who may not care
So much as grown-ups should do –

Cut flowers in vases rare –
Pottery rounded with these
(Best of all) or with no care   50
Ranged in may-hap degrees
In wide pot or any jar –
Gather them, pluck not, please.

I B Gurney
Stone House
Dartford
Kent
Appealing for Chance of Death
Pain of Life worse than Death

By Severn

If England, her spirit lives anywhere
It is by Severn, by hawthorns and grand willows.
Earth heaves up twice a hundred feet in air
And ruddy clay falls scooped out to the weedy shallows.
There in the brakes of May Spring has her chambers,   5
Robing-rooms of hawthorn, cowslip, cuckoo flower –
Wonder complete changes for each square joy's hour,
Past thought miracles are there and beyond numbers.
If for the drab atmospheres and managed lighting
In London town, Oriana's playwrights had   10
Wainlode her theatre and then coppice clad
Hill for her ground of sauntering and idle waiting.
Why, then I think, our chiefest glory of pride
(The Elizabethans of Thames, South and Northern side)
Would nothing of its needing be denied,   15
And her sons praises from England's mouth again be outcried.

Laventie

One would remember still
Meadows and low hill
Laventie was, as to the line and elm row
Growing through green strength wounded, as home elms
    grow.
Shimmer of summer there and blue autumn mists   5
Seen from trench-ditch winding in mazy twists.
The Australian gunners in close flowery hiding
Cunning found out at last, and smashed in the unspeakable
    lists.
And the guns in the smashed wood thumping and grinding.

The letters written there, and received there,   10
Books, cakes, cigarettes in a parish of famine,
And leaks in rainy times with general all-damning.
The crater, and carrying of gas cylinders on two sticks
(Pain past comparison and far past right agony gone,)
Strained hopelessly of heart and frame at first fix.   15

Café au lait in dugouts on Tommies cookers,
Cursed minnie werfs, thirst in 18 hour summer.
The Australian miners clayed, and the being afraid
Before strafes, sultry August dusk time than Death dumber –
And the cooler hush after the strafe, and the long night wait –   20
The relief of first dawn, the crawling out to look at it,
Wonder divine of Dawn, man hesitating before Heaven's
    gate.
(Though not on Coopers where music fire took at it,
Though not as at Framilode beauty where body did shake at
    it)
Yet the dawn with aeroplanes crawling high at Heaven's gate   25
Lovely aerial beetles of wonderful scintillate
Strangest interest, and puffs of soft purest white –
Soaking light, dispersing colouring for fancy's delight.

Of Maconachie, Paxton, Tickler, and Gloucester's Stephens;
Fray Bentos, Spiller and Baker, Odds and evens   30

Of trench food, but the everlasting clean craving
For bread, the pure thing, blessèd beyond saving.
Canteen disappointments, and the keen boy braving
Bullets or such for grouse roused surprisingly through
(Halfway) Stand-to.   35
And the shell nearly blunted my razor at shaving;
Tilleloy, Fauquissart, Neuve Chapelle, and mud like glue.

But Laventie, most of all, I think is to soldiers
The Town itself with plane trees, and small-spa air;
And vin, rouge-blanc, chocolats, citron, grenadine: 40
One might buy in small delectable cafés there.
The broken church, and vegetable fields bare;
Neat French market town look so clean,
And the clarity, amiability of North French air.
Like water flowing beneath the dark plough and high
    Heaven,   45
Music's delight to please the poet pack-marching there.

Canadians

We marched, and saw a company of Canadians
Their coats weighed eighty pounds at least, we saw them
Faces infinitely grimed in, with almost dead hands
Bent, slouching downwards to billets comfortless and dim.
Cave dwellers last of tribes they seemed, and a pity   5
Even from us just relieved (much as they were), left us.
Somme, what a desolation's damned land, what iniquity
Of mere being. There of what youth that country bereft us;
Plagues of evil lay in Death's Valley we also had
Forded that up to the thighs in chill mud almost still-stood   10
As they had gone – and endured day as night without sun.
Gone for five days then any sign of life glow
As the notched stumps or the gray clouds (then) we stood;
Dead past death from first hour and the needed mood
Of level pain shifting continually to and fro.   15

Saskatchewan, Ontario, Quebec, Stewart White ran in
My own mind; what in others? These men who finely
Perhaps had chosen danger for reckless and fine chance
Fate had sent for suffering and dwelling obscenely
Vermin eaten, fed beastly, in vile ditches meanly.   20
(Backwoods or clean Quebec for defiled, ruined, man-killing
    France
And the silver thrush no more crying Canada – Canada for the
    memory.

Of Cruelty

From the racked substance of the earth comes the plant and
That with heat and the night frost is tortured:
To some perfection that grows, man's thoughts wills his hand –
Roots rent, crown broken, grub holed, it is drawn upward.

A hundred things since the first stir have hunted it,   5
The rooks any time might have swallowed ungrateful,
Caterpillars, slugs, as it grew, have counted on it,
And man the planter bent his gaze down on it fateful.

The thing will go to market, it must be picked up and loaded,
The salesman will doubt it or chuck it anyway in,   10
A horse must be harnessed first, or a donkey goaded
Before the purchaser may ever the first price pay for it.

Who may be now trembling with vast impatience
And anxieties and mixed hopes for a resurrection
Out of the mouldering soul – to be new form, have perfections   15
Of flowers and petal and blade, to die, to be born to clean action.

The Cloud

One could not see or think, the heat overcame one,
With a dazzle of square road to challenge and blind one,
No water was there, cow parsley the only flower
Of all May's garland this torrid before-summer hour,
And but one ploughman to break ten miles of solitariness.   5
No water, water to drink, stare at, the lovely clean grained one.

Where like a falcon on prey, shadow flung downward
Solid as gun-metal, the eyes sprang sunward
To salute the silver radiance of an Atlantic high
Prince of vapour required of the retinue   10
Continual changing of the outer-sea's flooding sun
Cloud royal, born called and ordered to domination,
Spring called him out of his tent in the azure of pleasure,
He girt his nobleness – and in slow pace went onward
A true monarch of air chosen to service and station;   15
And directed on duties of patrolling the considered blue.
But what his course required being fulfilled, what fancy
Of beyond-imagination did his power escape to
With raiment of blown silver. . . .

Kilns

Severn has kilns set all along her banks
Where the thin reeds grow and rushes in ranks;
And the carts tip rubbish there from the town;
It thunders and raises white smoke and goes down.

I think some of those kilns are very old,   5
An age is on those small meres, and could unfold
Tales of many tenders of kilns and tales,
Of the diggers and earth delvers of those square weals
Or oblong of Severn bank. And all the flowers
June ever imagined stand and fulfil June's hours.   10
I think of the countless slabs gone out from all of them;
Farm house, cottage, loved of generations of men,
Fronting day as equal, or in dusk shining dim;
Of the Dane-folk curious of the sticky worthy stuff;
Kneading, and crumbling till the whim wearied enough.   15
Of the queer bricks unlearned hands must have made;
Spoiling clay, wasting wood, working out the war's trade;
With one hand the clear eyes fending, keeping in shade
Fierce Fire that grazes and melts with its regardings rough.
Or the plays children had of Dane-Saxon breed,   20
Chasing round the square kilns with devil-may-care
Headlong roughness of heedless body-reckless speed;
Grazing knees and knuckles to disaster there.
Of the creeping close to parents when November azure
Melancholy made company, and stillness, new pleasure,   25
And the wonder of fire kept the small boys to stay sure.

And the helping of fathers build well of the new brick,
The delight in handling over thin and thick – the youthful critic.

Of the Normans, how they liked kilns, that thrust to endure
Endless abbeys and strong chapels up in the air,   30
And Domesday questioners who worried the too evasive
Owner as to tales and days work to a story unplausive,
As to the fuels used, and the men there and the hours, the wage
   hours.

First Time In

After the dread tales and red yarns of the Line
Anything might have come to us; but the divine
Afterglow brought us up to a Welsh colony
Hiding in sandbag ditches, whispering consolatory
Soft foreign things. Then we were taken in   5
To low huts candle-lit shaded close by slitten
Oilsheets, and there but boys gave us kind welcome;
So that we looked out as from the edge of home.
Sang us Welsh things, and changed all former notions
To human hopeful things. And the next days' guns   10
Nor any line-pangs ever quite could blot out
That strangely beautiful entry to War's rout,
Candles they gave us precious and shared over-rations –
Ulysses found little more in his wanderings without doubt.
'David of the white rock', the 'Slumber Song' so soft, and that   15
Beautiful tune to which roguish words by Welsh pit boys
Are sung – but never more beautiful than here under the
     guns' noise.

La Gorgues

The long night, the short sleep, and La Gorgues to wander,
So be the Fates were kind and our Commander;
With a mill, and still canal, and like-Stroudway bridges.
One looks back on these as Time's truest riches –
Which were so short an escape, so perilous a joy –   5
Since fatigues, weather, Line trouble, or any whimsical play
Division might hatch out would have finished peace.

There was a house there – (I tell the noted thing)
The kindliest woman kept, and an unending string
Of privates as wasps to sugar went in and out.   10
Friendliness sanctified all there beyond doubt,

As lovely as the brick mill above the still green
Canal where the dark fishes went almost unseen.
Gloucester's B. Company had come down from Tilleloy, they
Lousy, thirsty, avid of any employ   15
Of peace; and this woman in leanest times had plotted
A miracle to amaze the army-witted – the time-cheated.
And this was café-au-lait as princes know it:
And fasting, and poor-struck; dead but not so as to show it,
A drink of epics, dooms, battles, a height of tales,   20
Rest, heat, cream, coffee; the maker tries and fails
The poet too, where such need such satisfaction had,
A campaign thing that makes keen remembrance sad.

It was light there, too, in the clear North French way,
It blessed the room and bread; and the mistress-giver . . .   25
The husband for his wife's sake, both for more than a day
Were blessed by many soldiers tired however, and forever
A mark in Time, a Peace, a Making-delay.
God bless the honourers of boy soldiers and the folk generous
Who dwell in light clean houses, and are glad to be thus   30
Serving France with love generous, in the light, clean house.

Blighty

It seemed that it were well to kiss first earth
On landing, having traversed the narrow seas,
And grasp so little, tenderly, of this field of birth.
France having trodden and lain on, travelled bending the
    knees.
And having shed blood – known heart for Her and last nerve
    freeze,   5
Proved body past heart, and soul past (so we thought) any
    worth
For what so dear a thing as the first homecoming,
The seeing smoke pillar aloft from the home dwellings;
Sign of travel ended, lifted awhile the dooming

Sentence of exile; homecoming, right of tale-tellings.   10
But mud is on our fate after so long acquaintance,
We find of England the first gate without Romance;
Blue paved wharfs with dock-policemen and civic decency,
Trains and restrictions, order and politeness and directions,
Motion by black and white, guided ever about ways   15
And staleness with petrol-dust distinguishing days.
A grim faced black-garbed mother efficient and busy
Set upon housework, worn-minded and fantasy free –
A work-house matron, forgetting Her old birth friend – the
     Sea.

Strange Hells

There are strange Hells within the minds War made
Not so often, not so humiliatingly afraid
As one would have expected – the racket and fear guns made.
One Hell the Gloucester soldiers they quite put out;
Their first bombardment, when in combined black shout   5
Of fury, guns aligned, they ducked lower their heads –
And sang with diaphrams fixed beyond all dreads,
That tin and stretched-wire tinkle, that blither of tune;
'Apres la guerre fini' till Hell all had come down.
12 inch – 6 inch and 18 pounders hammering Hell's
     thunders.   10

Where are They now on State-doles, or showing shop-
     patterns
Or walking town to town sore in borrowed tatterns
Or begged. Some civic routine one never learns.
The heart burns – but has to keep out of face how heart burns.

The Comparison

What Malvern is the day is, and it's touchstone
Gray velvet, or moonmarked; rich, or bare as bone;
One looks towards Malvern and is tuned to the whole,
The world swings round him, as the Bear to the Pole.

Men have crossed seas to know how Paul's tops Fleet;   5
So music has wrapt them high in the mere street
While none or few will care how the curved giants' stand,
(Those strengths upthrust!) on the meadow and plough-land.

But God wondered, when Wren heaved up Dome above
     Thames,
Worcestershire to Herefordshire Beacon learnt shapes and
     different names.   10
He is a Wonderer still, though men grow cold and chill –
And walk accustomed by Staunton or up Ludgate Hill.

Crucifix Corner

There was a water dump there, and regimental
Carts came every day to line up and fill full
Those rolling tanks with chlorinated clear mixture;
And curse the mud with vain veritable vexture.
Aveluy across the valley, billets, shacks, ruins,   5
With time and time a crump there to mark doings.
On New Year's Eve the marsh glowed tremulous
With rosy mist still holding late marvellous
Sun-glow, the air smelt home; the time breathed home.
Noel not put away; new term not yet come,   10
All things said 'Severn', the air was full of those calm
     meadows;
Transport rattled somewhere in the southern shadows;
Stars that were not strange ruled the most quiet high

Arch of soft sky, starred and most grave to see, most high.
What should break that but gun-noise or last Trump?   15
But neither came. At sudden, with light jump
Clarinet sang into 'Hundred Pipers and A' ',
Aveluy's Scottish answered with pipers true call
'Happy we've been a'together.' When nothing
Stayed of war-weariness or winter's loathing,   20
Crackers with Christmas stockings hung in the heavens,
Gladness split discipline in sixes and sevens,
Hunger ebb'd magically mixed with strange leavens;
Forgotten, forgotten the hard time's true clothing,
And stars were happy to see Man making Fate plaything.   25

I Saw England (July Night)

She was a village
Of lovely knowledge
The high roads left her aside, she was forlorn, a maid –
Water ran there, dusk hid her, she climbed four-wayed.
Brown-gold windows showed last folk not yet asleep;   5
Water ran, was a centre of silence deep,
Fathomless deeps of pricked sky, almost fathomless
Hallowed an upward gaze in pale satin of blue.
And I was happy indeed, of mind, soul, body even
Having got given   10
A sign undoubtful of a dear England few
Doubt, not many have seen,
That Will Squele he knew and was so shriven.
Home of Twelfth Night – Edward Thomas by Arras fallen,
Borrow and Hardy, Sussex tales out of Roman heights callen.   15
No madrigals or field-songs to my all reverent whim;
Till I got back I was dumb.

Poem For End

So the last poem is laid flat in its place,
And Crickley with Crucifix Corner leaves from my face
Elizabethans and night-working thoughts – of such grace.

And all the dawns that set my thoughts new to making;
Or Crickley dusk that the beech leaves stirred to shaking   5
Are put aside – there is a book ended; heart aching.

Joy and sorrow, and all thoughts a poet thinks,
Walking or turning to music; the wrought out links
Of fancy to fancy – by Severn or by Artois brinks.

Only what's false in this, blood itself would not save,   10
Sweat would not heighten – the dead Master in his grave
Would my true following of him, my care approve.

And more than he, I paid the prices of life
Standing where Rome immortal heard October's strife,
A war poet whose right of honour cuts falsehood like a knife.   15

War poet – his right is of nobler steel – the careful sword –
And night walker will not suffer of praise the word
From the sleepers; the custom-followers, the dead lives
    unstirred.

Only, who thought of England as two thousand years
Must keep of today's life, the proper anger and fears,   20
England that was paid for by building and ploughing and
    tears.

The Betrayal

Some men take a pride in honour –
Not I, so beaten by a witchcraft power
The hour grinds me, I lie beneath,
Helpless accusing to God each breath.

Not last determination may pride me,   5
Not any angel to stand beside me.
Beauty a torture of electrical like –
Music, their manner of my soul's spite.

The earth's glad things are terror to me,
Truth and endurance are error to me –   10
My county's tales, hidden or forgotten,
Are the way my heart is most thrice-broken.

God so absent, no blink but accuses
Of lighten-torture, his black arrogances
In creation, his wilfulness to men's hurt.   15
How shall our saints save against treacheries
Smuts-in-insult accusing the very earth's dirt.

Hell's Prayer

My God, the wind is rising! on those edges
Of Cotswold dark glory might swing my soul –
And Western Severn and North of water sedges
Mystery sounds, the wind's drums roll.
None will care to walk there. Those prefer to tell   5
Tales in a warm room of gossips, gettings, wages,
While I would be cursing exultant at the wind's toll
Of bell, shout of glory – swiftness of shadows.

My birth, my earning, my attained heritages
Ninety times denied me now thrust so far in Hell.   10

I think of the gods, all their old oaths and gages,
Gloucester has clear honour sworn without fail –
Companionship of meadows, high Cotswold ledges
Battered now tonight with huge wind-bursts and rages,
Flying moon glimpses like a shattered and flimsy sail –   15
In Hell I buried a score-depth, writing verse pages.

Masterpiece

Out from the dim mind like dark fires rises thought,
And one must be quick on it . . . or scratch sketches: a few. . . .
And later, three weeks later, in fashion sedater,
See, the night worker writing his square work out,
Set to the labour; muscle strained, his light hidden under: 5
Half past two? Time for tea . . . . half past, half past two. . . .
And then by degrees of half hours see how it shows:
The pages fill with black notes, the paper-bill goes
Up and up, till the musician is left staring
At a String Quartett nobody in the world will do. . . .   10
And what Schumann would say, there's no-one to be caring.
Now had it been a joke, or some wordy windy poem
About Destiny or Fatal-Way or Weltmüth or Sarsparilla;
London would have hugged to it like a glad gorilla . . .
Happy to know it's deepest heart told out so;   15
Deepest conviction, or maxim driven so home;
(To the next door neighbour.) But since the new making is
     still a
Mere Quartett for Strings after the Beethoven way,
With no aspiration to say more than ever was said
By Beethoven; expecting such treatment and casual pay;   20
the musician is left to turn over Shakespeare and to find
Favourite passages when the dim East shows blind.
Get rid of his drink how he may, blamed for such drinking.

Leave his MS there, wondering what neighbours may be
    thinking;
of people who work a week through without end.   25
And Neither Lyons, Lipton or the London String Quartett
To Care much what high glory from the light glory came to
    command.
Or – see . . . how the two tunes into one English picture came
    linking.

> With all respect
>   asking to print
>   sometimes.
>
> first go in
> Hell.
>   torture
>   and cold.
>
> *27th month.*

December 30th

It is the year's end, the winds are blasting, and I
Write to keep madness and black torture away
A little – it is a hurt to my head not to complain.
In the world's places that honour earth, all men are thinking
Of centuries: all men of the ages of living and drinking;   5
Singing and company of all time until now –
(When the hate of Hell has this England's state plain)
By the places I know this night all the woods are battering
With the great blast, clouds fly low, and the moon
(If there is any) clamorous, dramatic, outspoken.   10
In such nights as this Lassington has been broken,
Severn flooded too high and banks overflown –
And the great words of 'Lear' first tonight been spoken.
The boys of the villages growing up will say, 'I

Shall leave school, or have high wages, before another
    January –   15
Be grown up or free before again December's dark reign
Brightens to Christmas, dies for the old year's memory.'
May to them the gods make not all prayer's vain.

Cotswold Edge, Severn Valley that watches two
Magnificences; noble at right times or affectionate.   20
What power of these gods ever now call to you.
For the folks in you, of right noble; and of delight
In all Nature's things brought round in the years circle.
Pray God in blastings, supplicate now in terrifical
Tempestuous movings about the high-sided night.   25

Men I have known fine, are dead in France, in exile,
One my friend is dumb, other friends dead also,
And I that loved you, past the soul am in torture's spite
Cursing the hour that bore me, pain that bred all
My greater longings; Love only to you, this last-year date.   30

IV. January 1925–April 1926

March

My boat moves and I with her delighting,
Feeling the water slide past, and watching white fashion
Of water, as she moves faster ever more whitening;
Till up at the white sail in that great sky heightening
Of fine cloth spread against azure and cloud commotion   5
My face looks, and there is joy in the eyes that asking
Fulfilment of the heart's true and golden passion
(Long dimmed) now gets hold of a truth and an action. . . .
The ears take the sound of Severn water dashing.
The great spirit remembers Ulysses with his courage lighting 10
Before the danger of sea water, in a rocky passion
Of surges – and over Barrow comes the wind I've been waiting.

The Sea Borders

Well I know though I have not seen how the white edges
Of the sea make fury now by Devon or Maryland –
What grand spirit batters uselessly against old Brittany,
Or against Hebrides with black granite wedges
Of Rock. And all the writers who have ever written the   5
Annals of seafaring will tell me little more
Of how the water at a huge ship's onset surges
Than my own little boat's prow sailing Severn recklessly.
(But O those great three masters of the past ages!)

Tales told in the foc'sle, or hauling hand over hand   10
Hauling on ropes, the companionship in close quarters –
The lovely shocks of beauty of the noises of broken waters . . .
These I have known, not because writers made tales to
    command
My shame and glory, and terror all clear to me.
Not because my life has had soldiership and greatest labour of
    body. . . .   15
Not because only I have been all mens' all women's friend.
But because I musician have wrestled with the stuff in
    making,
And wrought a square thing out of my stubborn mind –
And gathered a huge surge of spirit as the great barriers bind
The whole Atlantic at them by Devon or West Ireland.   20

The Love Song

Out of the blackthorn edges
I caught a tune
And before it could vanish, seized
It, wrote it down.

Gave it to a girl, so praising   5
Her eyes, lips and hair
She had little knowing, it was only thorn
Had dreamed of a girl there.

Prettily she thanked me, and never
Guessed any of my deceit. . . .   10
But O Earth is this the only way
Man may conquer, a girl surrender her sweet?

Snow

There's not a sound to-night.
I look out and am beaten
In my face by curious, white,
Unexpected flakes
Of snow in a daze fleeting.   5

And retire shivering to
The warm room and the lamplight,
Where my music waits, and O
Ben Jonson lies. . . . .
For delight my man's nature with his great spirit.   10

O warmth! O Golden light!
O books behind me waiting
Their turn for my love's thought. . . .
Turning from work
To wrap myself in a past of golden lighting.   15

Music must flow with his power, I
Bend over my task and am hard
At wrestling with the stuff for mastery
That is dumb music now –
My spirit and I wrestle, you may hear us breathing hard.   20

Was there any Love, could draw me
Out of my true way of work and action?
Yes, one there was, but Time has dared show me
(A soldier and maker)
That Time dares all things, and defies ever question.   25

Thoughts on Beethoven

Beethoven I wronged thee undernoting thus
Thy dignity and worth; the overplus
Of one quartett almost would our book overweigh –
Almost chosen out at random from your own day.
You have our great Ben's mastery and a freer   5
Carriage of method, spice of the open air. . . . .
Which he our greatest builder had not so:
Not as his own at least, but acquiréd-to.
May no false fashion put thy true fame away
As in Vienna, when wantons laid all away   10
Thy work Homeric for a soft Southern zephyr –
And heroes were no other than as day's heifer
Sacrificed on the altar of worlds praise;
The amusement or brittle heightening of drab days.

Whereas thy sinewed strength is by Aeschylus   15
Homer, Ben Jonson, Shakespeare and a pillar of us.
Master. Such are our memories which do never betray
Our own makings, Thou so generous in thy great-heart way.

First poem

O what will you turn out, book, to be?
Who are not my joy, but my escape from the worst
And most accurst of my woe? Shall you be poetry,
Or tell truth, or be of past things the tale rehearsed?

Thoughts

Watching the books before me in my dazed pain,
Chaucer and Ballads, 'Leaves of Grass', 'Voces Intimae' –
Dazed with torture still, with never a real let in pain, –
I know the black wrong London eternally plots against me –
Who have right of Her great honour, and to ask without
     denying.   5
See, there is Petit de Julleville, and Mozart's Quartetts,
Robert Bridges (in queer black binding that repels and hurts)
Most honoured, and Shakespeare master of free writing poet's
     Company.
(The Ballads, which opened, give a clang out like great iron.)
But all the torture weighs so heavy on all my days,   10
It is an effort to read even Francis Jammes with heed –
Chaucer is an almost false and mind-supported praise.
I who in the Line read, (lousy) worried with deaths and dirts,
Aeschylus, Keats and Ronsard stretched lazy in signaller
     wise, –
Get no more good of scholarship than an anguish defying   15
All love, all glory, all hope of making my true own;
And the City has done this, to most honour being bound
     inevitably. . . .
London; It is London – the old golden City; it is the Hell called
     London.

Like Hebridean

Great sea water surged to its green height of white,
Clamouring in the stone arch, ages on ages all
Had made – Turning at last to seas's natural delight,
Water from the deep playing first its great free game here.
(Zennor Head grim it was, granite of old Cornwall.)   5
So long the Sea had been toy thing to hearing and sight,
After great poetry music – it was mere relief great
To watch and hear rage of sea water hammering on granite
    stone here.
So, the Sagas were not lies, Chanties, and certain loved
    music . . .
Men had told truth. December in strong despite   10
Battered with wind and water old County of Cornwall.
(Seagulls uttering drear, flying momently, their strange call.)
Until now ploughland hard kept my truth; colour, mystery of
    ground,
Rise to hide heaven of earth, or sudden white or green fall;
Before this tame thing, Sea, was honoured for all virtue.   15
Yet now the white uptossing surge, great hoarse-voiced
    sound,
Compelled admiration – surf in leagues all of elation. . . .
The Poets were not liars, here also was glory to praised and
    found.

The Strange thing

Coming free out of 3 weeks trenches they cheered –
(The Gloucesters) weak and hungry as winter rabbits, –
    starved
For tea, or wine or sitting warm smoking easy by a fire –
They cheered, and I laughed, and got a short moment's fire.
What was it? A girl, we had seen never any woman for   5
Six weeks or so, and had been strafed and stood sentry frore

Watching over to Chaulnes in evil dark unstarred:
Stepping out from breakfast into three foot frosted water;
(The worst time all of France – far worse than we had feared.)
And so this sight of France, this kind-heart daughter   10
Of the land that writes clear poetry and fought fierce
    Wattignies –
We welcomed as though Cotswold suddenly here had
    appeared;
(smiling) With our own girls, above Artois flat plain here –
Would have broken ranks to kiss her, if we dared had
    dared. . . .
So Gloucester caught at lost humanity like old Gloucester.   15

Epitaph on a Young Child

They will bury that fair body and cover you –
You shall be no more seen of the eyes of men,
Not again shall you search the woodlands, – not ever again
For violets – the wind shall be no more dear lover of you.

Other children shall grow as fair, but not so dear,   5
And the cold spirited shall say 'It is wrong that the body
Should be so beautiful' – O puritans warped to moody!
You were the true darling of the earth of your shire.

And all the flowers you touched, but would for pity not pick,
In the next Spring shall regret you and on and so on –   10
Whether you are born again your love shall not be done –
In the most wonderful April or October your spirit be mystic.

Dear body (it is an evil age) that so enclosed
So lovely a spirit, generous, quick to anothers small pain;
Is it true you in the dark earth must be down-lain?   15
Are there no more smiles from you in the *house*, sunlight
    drowsed?

I must find out a Love to console my hurt loneliness,
Forget your children's beauty in the conflict of days –
Until there come to me also the sweetness of some boy's
Or girl's beauty – a Western spirit in a loved coloured dress of
    flesh.   20

Christopher Marlowe

With all that power he died, having done (his) nothing. . . .
And none of us are safe against such terrible proving
That time puts on men – Such power shown; so little
    done. . . .
Then the earth shut him out from the light of the sun.
All his tears, all his prayers to God, and Elizabethan loving   5
Gone to a nothing, before he was well of age –
Having seen Cornwall, perhaps visited a loved Germany,
(Gloucester will send heart out to like Canterbury,
In the maker's heart was some likeness of clear striving)
Known all London, read in many a poets page –   10
Brave and generous, braggart and generous in doing,
Poet born and soldier, sobering to his elder age;
The earth covered him and wrought wood was his clothing.
'Tamburlaine' half glorious, then 'Faustus', half victorious,
He left us, chief, an ache that a poet true man of men,   15
Should be stabbed cold, like any mean half gallant frothing;
    nothing,
Other men honoured, great ones made a tradition true,
But we curse luck for silence in manners various –
The courage and youth and virtue of Christopher Marlowe.

Song of Autumn

Music is clear about such freshness and colour,
   But how shall I get it?
There is great joy in walking to the quarry scar,
   And glory – I have had it.

Beech woods have given me truest secrets, and the sighing   5
Firs I know, have told me
Truth of the hearts of children, the lovers of making.
Old camps have called me.

It is time I should go out to ways older than tales,
Walk hard, and return   10
To write an evening and a night through with so many wills
Aiding me – little now to learn.

The Last of the book

There is nothing for me, Poetry, who was the child of joy,
But to work out in verse crazes of my untold pain;
In verse which shall recall the rightness of a former day.

And of Beauty, that has command of many gods; in vain
Have I written, imploring your help, who have let destroy   5
A servant of yours, by evil men birth better at once had slain.

And for my Country, God knows my heart, Land, men to me
Were dear there, I was friend also of very look of sun or rain;
It has betrayed as evil women wantonly a man their toy.

Soldiers' praise I had earned having suffered soldier's pain,   10
And the great honour of song in the battle's first gray show –
Honour was bound to me save mine most dreadfully stain.

Rapt heart, once, hills I wandered alone, joy was comrade
    there, though
Little of what I needed, was in my power: again – again
Hours I recall, dazed with pain like a still weight set to my
    woe.   15

Blood, birth, long remembrance, my County, all these have
    saven
Little of my being from dreadfullest hurt, the old gods have no
Pity – or long ago I should have got good, they would have
    battled my high right plain.

Butchers and Tombs

After so much battering of fire and steel
It had seemed well to cover them with Cotswold stone –
And shortly praising their courage and quick skill
Leave them buried, hidden till the slow, inevitable
Change came should make them service of France alone –   5
But the times hurry the commonness of the tale
Made it a thing not fitting ceremonial,
And so the disregarders of blister on heel,
Pack on shoulder, barrage and work at the wires,
One wooden cross had for ensign of honour and life gone –   10
Save when the Gloucesters turning sudden to tell to one
Some joke, would remember and say – 'That joke is done.'
Since he who would understand was so cold he could not feel,
And clay binds hard, and sandbags get rotten and crumble.

Serenade

It was after the Somme, our line was quieter,
Wires mended, neither side daring attacker
Or aggressor to be – the guns equal, the wires a thick hedge,
Where there sounded, (O past days for ever confounded!)
The tune of Schubert which belonged to days mathematical, 5
Effort of spirit bearing fruit worthy, actual.
The gramophone for an hour was my quiet's mocker,
Until I cried, 'Give us Heldenleben', 'Heldenleben',
The Gloucesters cried out 'Strauss is our favourite wir haben
Sich geliebt'. So silence fell, Aubers front slept, 10
And the sentries an unsentimental silence kept.
True, the size of the rum ration was still a shocker
But at last over Aubers the majesty of the dawn's veil swept.

Don Juan in Hell

I heard a soldier tell, frozen out of all patience,
Tales of girls he had kissed, whose bodies touched, when a
    trench
Was a name of potatoes, gun a thing for crows,
And Somme a river, distant far, by no chance to be his.
But pained to talk, he told me how one had kissed 5
Him out of anger before his anger was wist,
Another his impudence out of all harm, by charm. . . .
It was the talk of Shakespeare – the sound of a farm –
Gossip before the world by fire was turned bitter and spurned
All that the day's labour in sin had earned. 10
'Now that I've stood my turn, and have right of all
I ask, I wonder what end – if it come – will befall
My asking – O at least; not the last
Battle, not the last day of all.'

The Bohemians

Certain people would not clean their buttons,
Nor polish buckles after latest fashions,
Preferred their hair long, putties comfortable,
Barely escaping hanging, indeed hardly able,
In Bridge and smoking without army cautions   5
Spending hours that sped like evil for quickness,
(While others burnished brasses, earned promotions)
These were those ones who jested in the trench,
While others argued of army ways, and wrenched
What little soul they had still further from shape,   10
And died off one by one, or became officers
Without the first of dream, the ghost of notions
Of ever becoming soldiers, or smart and neat,
Surprised as ever to find the army capable
Of sounding 'Lights out' to break a game of Bridge,   15
As to fear candles would set a barn alight.
In Artois or Picardy they lie – free of useless fashions.

To Long Island First

To Long Island first with my tortured verse,
Remember how on a Gloucester book-stall one morning
I saw, brown 'Leaves of Grass' after long hesitation
(For fourpence to me was bankruptcy then or worse).
I bought, what since in book or mind about the dawning   5
On Roman Cotswold, Roman Artois war stations;
Severn and Buckingham, London after night wanderings,
Has served me, friend or Master on many occasions,
Of weariness, or gloriousness or delight.
At first to puzzle, then grow past all traditions   10
To be Master unquestioned – a book that brings the clear
Spirit of him that wrote, to the thought again here.

If I have not known Long Island none has –
Brooklyn is my own City, Manhattan the right of me,
Camden and Idaho – and all New England's   15
Two-fold love of honour, honour and comely grace.
If blood to blood can speak or the spirit has inspiring,
Let me claim place there also – Briton I am also Hers,
And Roman, have more than Virgil for meditations.

The New Poet

Out of the dark North and the easy South –
One with Saga strung against the bitter cold;
The other with happiness and homely songs of gold;
Let there be born a new poet – and let him sing
Of all the States, let his home be the Town watching   5
Mississippi flowing southward with names untold,
And waters numberless hidden in Her flowing.
More honouring masters old than one Walt Whitman,
Nor like Longfellow falling from his true matching
Of the nobility of earth with the nobility of words –   10
But out of Greece, Rome, Middle England and the all
    honouring
Provinces of France, and the Indian tradition,
A new poetry of all lights, all times; wherein swords
Are not honoured more than the shares ploughing
The coloured earth to furrows, dry or wet shards.   15
Let him say all men's thought nor sleep until
Some great thing he has fashioned of love inevitable.
For the rest, may he follow his happiness' true will.

Signallers

To be signallers and to be relieved two hours
Before the common infantry – and to come down
Hurriedly to where estaminets friendliest doors
Opened – where before the vulgar brawling common crew
Could take the seats for tired backs, or take the wine   5
Best suited for palates searching for delicate flavours
(Or pretty tints) to take from the mind trench ways and strain,
Though it be on tick, with delicately wangled sly favours.
Then having obtained grace from the lady of the inn –
How good to sit still and sip with all-appreciative lip,   10
(After the grease and skilly of line-cookhouse tea.)
The cool darkling texture of the heavenly dew
Of wine – to smoke as one pleased in a house of courtesy –
Signallers gentlemen all away from the vulgar
Infantry – so dull and dirty and so underpaid,   15
So wont to get killed and leave the cautious signallers
To signal down the message that they were dead.
Anyway, distinctions or not – There was a quiet
Hour or so before the Company fours halted, and were
Formed two deep, and dismissed and paid after leaden
    dilatory   20
Hanging around, to bolt (eager) to find those apparently
Innocent signallers drinking on tick, at last beer.

It is near Toussaints

It is near Toussaints, the living and dead will say,
'Have they ended it? what has happened to Gurney?'
And along the leafstrewed roads of France many brown
  shades
Will go, recalling singing, and a comrade for whom also they
Had hoped well. His honour them had happier made.   5
Curse all that hates good. When I spoke of my breaking

(not understood) in London, they imagined of the taking
Vengeance, and seeing things were different in future.
(A musician was a cheap, honourable and nice creature.)
Kept sympathetic silence; heard their packs creaking   10
And burst into song – Hilaire Belloc was all our Master.
On the night of the dead, they will remember me,
Pray Michael, Nicholas, Maries lost in Novembery
River-mist in the old City of our dear love, and batter
At doors about the farms crying 'Our war poet is lost'   15
'Madame, no bon' – and cry his two names, warningly,
    sombrely.

Song

I had a girl's fancies
At the pools –
And azure at chances
In the rut holes
Minded me of Maisemore,   5
And Gloucester men
Beside me made sure
All faithfulness again.

The man's desiring
Of great making   10
Was denied; and breaking
To the heart much-caring –
Only the light thoughts
Of the poet's range
Stayed in that war's plights.   15
Only soul did not change.

So to the admiration
Of the rough high virtues
Of common marching
Soldier; and textures   20

Of russet noblenesses
My mind was turned
But where are such verses
That in my heart burned?

The Mangel-bury

It was after War, Edward Thomas had fallen at Arras –
I was walking by Gloucester musing on such things
As fill his verse with goodness; It was February; the long house
Straw-thatched of the mangels stretched two wide wings;
And looked as part of the earth heaped up by dead soldiers   5
In the most fitting place – along the hedges yet-bare-lines.
West spring breathed there early, that none foreign divines.
Across the flat country the rattling of the cart sounded;
Heavy of wood, jingling of iron; as he neared me, I waited
For the chance perhaps of heaving at those great rounded   10
Ruddy Or orange things – and right to be rolled and hefted
By a body like mine, soldier-still, and clean from water.
Silent he assented; till the cart was drifted
High with those creatures, so right in size and matter,
We threw them with our bodies swinging; blood in my ears singing: 15
His was the thick-set sort of farmer, but well-built –
Perhaps long before, his blood's name ruled all:
Watched all things for his own. If my luck had so willed
Many questions of lordship I had heard him tell – old
Names, rumours. But my pain to more moving called   20
And him to some barn business far in the fifteen acre field.

'They have left me little indeed'

They have left me little indeed, how shall I best keep
Memory from sliding content down to drugged sleep?
But my blood in its colour even is known fighter –
If I were hero for such things here I would make wars
As love for dead things trodden under Januarys stars.   5

Or the gold trefoil itself spending in careless places
Tiny graces like music's for its past exquisitenesses.
Why war for huge Domains of the planet's heights or plains.
(Little they leave me.) It is a dream, hardly my heart dares
Tremble for glad leaf-drifts thundering under January's stars.   10

The Depths

Here no dreams touch me to colour
Sodden state of all-dolour:
No touch of peace, no creation
Felt, nor stir of divination.

Friend of stars, things, inky pages –   5
Knowing so many heritages
Of Britain old, or Roman newer;
Here all witchcrafts scar and skewer.

Coloured maps of Europe taking
And words of poets fine in making,   10
I march once more with hurt shoulders,
And scent the air, a friend with soldiers.

Devil's dooms that none guess,
Evil's harms worshipped no less
Grind my soul – and no god clutches   15
Out of darks god's-honour smutches.

Early Winter

I love chrysanthemums and winter jasmine,
Clustering lichened walls a century old;
That in my Western ways when days draw in,
Grow in the farm gardens in the first cold.
Strange foreigners should prove   5
So homely to my love.

For all the age that lies upon this land
Seems to call out for things native, things like
Britain knew, when the tongue talked soft, and
Not yet Rome from the far Gaul might strike.   10
Yet here Japan
Has flowered as after plan.

Farewell

What! to have had gas, and to expect
No more than a week's sick, and to get Blighty –
This is the gods' gift, and not anyway exact –
To Ypres, or bad St Julien or Somme Farm.
Don Hancocks, shall I no more see your face frore,   5
Gloucester-good, in the first light? (But you are dead!)
Shall I see no more Monger with india rubber
Twisted Face – (But machine gun caught him and his
    grimace.)
No more to march happy with such good comrades,
Watching the sky, the brown land, the bayonet blades.   10
Moving – to muse on music forgetting the pack.
Nor to hear Gloucester with Stroud debating the lack
Of goodliness or virtue in girls on farmlands.
Nor to hear Cheltenham hurling at Cotswold demands
Of civilisation; nor West Severn joking at East Severn? 15
No more – across the azure or brown lands

The morning mist, or high day clear of rack,
Shall move my dear knees – or feel them frosted, shivering
By Somme and Aubers – or to have a courage from faces
Full of all West England, Her God gives graces.　　　　　　20
There was not one of all that Battalion
Loved his comrades as well as I – but kept shy.
Or said in verse, what his voice would not rehearse.
So gassed I went back – to Northlands where voices speak soft
　　　as in verse.
And after to meet evil not fit for the thought one touch to
　　　dwell on.　　　　　　25
Dear Battalion, the dead of you would not have let
your comrade be so long-prey for the unquiet
Black evil of the unspoken and concealed pit.
You would have had me safe – dead or free happy alive.
They bruise my head and torture with their own past-hate　　30
Sins of the past, and lie so as earth moves at it –
You dead ones – I lay with you under the unbroken wires
　　　once.

The Sudden Storm

Who but I walked the hills to see the lightning,
Say the few remembered things of Lear – the harried King,
Royal in his words, royal in his foul ruining.
Lightning at Framilode – and by Laventie trenches.
On Chilterns, and surely Cotswold – surely I have gone,　　5
By road and rabbit run under the sudden sword shine;
Surely from Coopers and from Crickley the heavens have seen
　　　open?
But men have ceased reverence – and not honour those,
Braver or more bright of spirit who have hurried to the ways
Where great sound and great light fell in avalanches,　　10
Flat on the open slopes – or kept off by the branches.
Glorying the spirit to fulness, and great gladness of dark days.

(Beethoven shouting the delight out of the heart in high
    amaze.)
But West of Ypres we lying blanketed in the dark,
A sudden glow from Dunkerque made wonder, and the
    work –   15
And hunger-tired body rose up to guess at such storm,
Making no sound, in the September night calm and warm.
But next days papers told us, it was an electrical
Storm, for goodness knows what purpose let loose at all.
And no landing – or bombardment, or cause of excitement.   20
Anyway, sleep; but no sleep for me possible there was
When the great electricity burst out in blaze,
By Chilterns, or Crickley Hill, or flat Longford's ways.

Ben Jonson

Few have praised the master of masters, who but I
Have right, that followed example, and did not lie
Idly between clean sheets when was work to do.
And saw Paul's tower by Embankment, high over City in dew
Not resolved; sunlight of hidden sun; and with apprentices   5
Drank, and watched faces in Whitefrairs Lane, to my fancies.
Such work tops all but of Shakespeare, the earths child, the
    sun's,
He of no fairy gift, but of hard-first resolutions –
And set to build as Bartholemews lover that Saint –
Or Wren in a later day raising great stone from the burnt   10
History and heart's love of the City London.
(So much merchants', scholars love so dreadfully undone.)
But if not I, that have praised in music his town
Worthy of his praise – and to glory made great stone known.
If not I that of Embankment and Aldgate wrote –   15
The Age is mean indeed, and honours only by rote.
Chapman, and Marston, Ford, Shirley, marks to frighten;
To frighten those, whom their example should urge and
    heighten.

The age is honourless, and my walking in loneliness.
My long thoughts in strict ways, my work – followings of him,   20
Are scorn to those whose lives are a wind breadth's whim.
Follow nor good nor evil – see not, with eyes custom dim.

Of Grandcourt

Through miles of mud we travelled, and by sick valleys –
The Valley of Death at last – most evil alleys.
To Grandcourt trenches reserve – and the hells name it did
    deserve
Rain there was – Tired and weak I was, glad for an end.
But one spoke to me – one I liked well as friend –   5
'Lets volunteer for the Front line – many others wont'.
'I'll volunteer – its better being there than here'.
But I had seen too many ditches and stood too long
Feeling my feet freeze, and my shoulders ache with the strong
Pull of equipment – and too much use of pain and strain   10
Besides he was Lance Corporal and might be full Corporal,
Before the next straw resting might come again.
Before the next billet should hum with talk and song.
Stars looked as well from second as from first line holes.
There were fatigues for change, and a thought less danger –   15
But five or six there were followed Army with their souls –
Took five days dripping rain without let or finish again –
With dysentery and bodys of heroic ghouls.
Till at last their hearts feared nothing of the brazen anger,
(Perhaps of death little) but once more again to drop on straw
    bed-serving   20
And to have heaven of dry feeling after the damps and fouls.

The Silent One

Who died on the wires, and hung there, one of two –
Who for his hours of life had chattered through
Infinite lovely chatter of Bucks accent;
Yet faced unbroken wires; stepped over, and went,
A noble fool, faithful to his stripes – and ended.   5
But I weak, hungry, and willing only for the chance
Of line – to fight in the line, lay down under unbroken
Wires, and saw the flashes, and kept unshaken.
Till the politest voice – a finicking accent, said:
'Do you think you might crawl through there; there's a hole';
   In the afraid   10
Darkness, shot at; I smiled, as politely replied –
'I'm afraid not, Sir.' There was no hole, no way to be seen,
Nothing but chance of death, after tearing of clothes
Kept flat, and watched the darkness, hearing bullets
   whizzing –
And thought of music – and swore deep heart's deep oaths.   15
(Polite to God –) and retreated and came on again.
Again retreated – and a second time faced the screen.

Elizabethans

Shakespeare was my friend (feared) at sixteen years.
Johnson 'the Alchemist' at twenty two or so.
Beaumont and Fletcher, Marlowe next my gain –
Puzzled making out the reputation of a masters show.
And never finding it, and never finding it.   5
There was 'Roaring Girl' and of 'the Golden West'
But not till London was made manifest
In one short summer the fat works of Ben Jonson,
Half a crown, and Morley half a crown.
Then I knew delight, then masters in the late night   10
I had, new pride, and Beethoven put aside –

For Marston, Shirley, Greene, and Ford my delight.
Who'd feed my fill, and go to muse on them
By Westminster or stray lanes of City by Thames –
(Knowing why my blood held of life such high mood,   15
Knowing why makers kept watch of high star acres;
And why the unresting spirit to me was good.)
Putting aside the greatest of song with gladness,
For the strong manliness of the Great Company of play-
  writers.
Who had their job, and took delight, deep till midnight.   20
Verse of clear wonder, out of earth love brought to arts-right.
But none have helped me. Deep to Hell Gloucester let betray
  me.
Pain no word can say of me. Hell has racked me, and God not
  helped me.

Portrait of a Coward

True he'd have fought to death if the Germans came –
But an hours battering after a days battering
Brought his soul down to quivering, with small shame.
And he was fit to run, if his chance had come.
But Gloucesters of more sterner frame and spirit   5
Kept him in place without reproach, (sweet blood inherit
From hills and nature) said no word and kept him there.
True, he'd have fought to death, but Laventie's needing
Was a nerve to hide the pain of his soul bleeding –
Say nothing, and nothing ever of God to beg.   10
He hurt more, did fatigues, and was friend to share
What food was not his need; of enemies not heeding.
Everybody was glad – (but determined to hide the bad)
When he took courage at wiremending and shot his leg,
And got to Blighty, no man saying word of denying.   15

War books

What did they expect of our toil and extreme
Hunger – the perfect drawing of a hearts dream?
Did they look for a book of wrought art's perfection,
Who promised no reading, nor praise, nor publication?
Out of the heart's sickness the spirit wrote.   5
For delight, or to escape hunger, or of war's worst anger.
When the guns died to silence, and men would gather sense
Somehow together, and find this was life indeed.
And praise another's nobleness, or to Cotswold get hence.
There we wrote – Corbie Ridge – or in Gonnehem at rest.   10
Or Fauquissart or worlds death songs ever the best.
One made sorrows praise passing the church where silence
Opened for the long quivering strokes of the bell –
Another wrote all soldiers praise, and of France and night's
    stars –
Served his guns, got immortality, and died well.   15
But Ypres played another trick with its danger on me,
Kept still the needing and loving of action body;
Gave no candles, and nearly killed me twice as well.
And no souvenirs though I risked my life in the stuck Tanks.
Yet there was praise of Ypres, love came sweet in hospital –   20
And old Flanders went under to long ages of plough thought
    in my pages.

V. September 1926–March 1929

the Shelter from the Storm

And meantime fearing snow the flocks are brought in,
They are in the barn where stone tiles and wood shelter
From the harm shield; where the rosy-faced farmers daughter
Goes to visit them.

She pats and fondles all her most favourite first.   5
then after that the shivering and unhappy ones –
Spreads hay, looks up at the noble and gray roof vast
And says 'This will stop storms'.

Her mind is with her books in the low-ceilinged kitchen
Where the twigs blaze. – and she sees not sheep alone   10
of the Cotswold, but in the Italian shelters songs repeating
Herdsmen kind, from the blast gone.

I read now so

So I read now, dull verse in hidden measures –
Great of the earth or earldom, or of abbeys –
So I listen now or scan to find great pageant treasures:
Fall in infinite depths of terror, heights of Hell.
Love all persuading, powerful, tender infinite –   5
of the worlds, blessed Mary's children's, friends
And then again my verse or the verse of my friend.
By a City or a library, or in post betrayed.
Stolen else, to be a pride of a torturer in torture.
The devils barren to cheat the rich right forepaid.   10

Ruin and empty work made of our fine,
Our fine work signed under another's trade –
and the Master of us all a trap; corrupted made
A peril for boys, a book for the cunning, that's said
To be the tender and high book of England's drawing –   15
Terrible and secret, when rich asking pain over-paid.
Danger in masters, and slick thieves at the trade.
So read I now, on thin ice or on spiked reserve to go,
As leave my thoughts of County or of music's bounty –
The spear of the gods bent in a trident and a bow   20
To shoot the poisoned arrow unmoving frozen shining slow.

Near Spring

Now the strong horse goes loose at last,
Free for his strength, in the February's end –
Floods have left the meadows and gone past
To the broader rivers rocks and sand.

Musing on old tunes, ploughboys go   5
Hoping to catch the lilt forgot
Of a tune their fathers recalled in glow
of talking, or after cricket hot.

The year stirs wing and watches skies
Deep-in again; the girl is happy   10
With her white apron showing in the doorway's
Frame; daffodills thrill in hedgebanks ruddy.

Sea-Marge

Pebbles are beneath, but we stand softly
On them, as on sand, and watch the lacy edge
of the swift sea.

Which patterns and with glorious music the
Sands and round stones – It talks ever   5
Of new patterns.

And by the cliff-edge, there, the oakwood throws
A shadow deeper to watch what new thing
Happens at the marge.

the Bridge

Ceremony that the boys loved is no more
About those white walls fallen –
Nor will any
At all-Hallows even cry out Humphrey's ensigns.

At the gate none will praise the well wrought   5
Heraldry of the long bridge sun-silver all-honour –
A dirty water drifts between crampt
Borders, lies and goes past the shadow.

In far ravines and on heights love delights in
the trees will pity the haggard Half-Lady   10
Of crystal-sprung Severn
The flowers beneath accuse angels betraying

the dancers

the dancers danced in a quiet meadow
It was winter, the soft light lit in clouds
Of growing morning – their feet on the firm
Hill-side sounded like a baker's business
Heard from the yard of his beamy barn-grange.   5
One piped, and the measured irregular riddle
Of the dance ran onward in tangling threads. . . .
A thing of the village centuries old in charm.
With tunes from the earth they trod, and naturalness
Sweet like the need of pleasure of change.   10
For a lit room with panels gleaming
they practised this set by winter's dreaming
Of pictures as lovely as are in Spring's range. . . .
No candles, but the keen dew-drops shining. . . .
And only the far jolly barking of the dog strange.   15

Musers afar will say

Soon will blow the changed leaves on the Malvern road
Hurtling in tiny charge: and the streams will be strowed
With arrows and shields of a hundred affectionate fields. . . . .
But who to dear desiring Gloucester will bring good?

Men afar off by strange rivers will say 'Now the year   5
Will be storming and crying triumphant before death there
By Gloucester.' But who will bring Severn any hearts good,
Full heralded bright river? They will fear, and they'll remember.

the Pedlars Song

Now dust is on the roads,
And the blue hills call to distances,
On my shoulders I take my fancies
And travel where good shows . . .
To places of gray stone and water   5
Where a squire and his lovely daughter
Come once to talk with old Richard Spragg
And give tea, for the heart's glows.

The squire with his old right
And the lady with half a bookful   10
Of names for homages delight
They are my patrons and like-council –
I travel through frosty weather warming
the blood that shall lie in a barn at evening –
And that's their bounty with farm hands company,   15
The blaze and converse of nightfall.

I never travel without
A pipe for company, nor books
Of tunes that delight heart –
And ancient honest wood-cuts –   20
Skill enough but there's love in my fingers –
The harpsichord is served by my prayers, –
And many a house and manor of music
Has learnt from my crammed pack.

In sweet lands making travel,   25
With money for taverns, at lucks time
Or to lie on the straw with a double
Roof on my head, hostel of rhyme. . . .
And never a rough word from seven demesnes,
For I carry them treasures they'd else miss –   30
Till I die, I will serve Middle Ages honour;
Then die, and be a faithful name.

I would not rest

I would not rest till work came from my hand. . . .
And then the thing grew, till fame came,
(But only in honour) . . . And then O how the grand
Divination of ages grew to faith's flame. . . . . .
Great were our fathers and beautiful in all name.   5
Happy their days, lovely in considered grain each word.
Their days were kindness, growth, happiness mindless. . . .

I would not rest until my County were
Thronged with the Halls of Music; and until clear
Hospitality for love were ere possible. . . .   10
And any for honour might come, or prayer, to certain
Fondness and long nights' talking till all's known.

Madness my enemy, cunning extreme my friend,
Prayer my safeguard. (Ashes my reward at end.)
Secrecy fervid my honour. Soldier-courage my aid –   15
(Promise and evil threatening my soul ever-afraid)
Now, with the work long done, to the witchcraft I bend
And crouch – that knows nothing good, Hell uncaring
Hell undismayed.

'Soft rain beats upon my windows'

Soft rain beats upon my windows
Hardly hammering.
But by the great gusts guessed further off
Up by the bare moor and brambly headland
Heaven and earth make war.   5

That savage toss of the pine boughs past music
And the roar of the elms. . . .
Here come, in the candle light, soft reminder

Of poetry's truth, while rain beats as softly here
As sleep, or shelter of farms.   10

The Wind

All night the fierce wind blew –
All night I knew
Time, like a dark wind, blowing
All days, all lives, all memories
Down empty endless skies –   5
A blind wind, strowing
Bright leaves of life's torn tree
through blank eternity:
Dreadfully swift, Time blew.
All night I knew   10
the outrush of its going.

At dawn a thin rain wept.
Worn out, I slept
And woke to a fair morning.
My days were amply long, and I content   15
In their accomplishment –
Lost the wind's warning.

Valentine Fane

Notes

Listed below are the sources for the texts reproduced here, followed by information as to their possible dates. References that appear only once in this selection are annotated in the entries to individual poems; multiple refernces, such as those to Ben Jonson or Walt Whitman, are annotated in the Glossary that follows this section.

I. July 1915–1919

p.3 To the Poet before Battle: (*Severn & Somme*, 1917) sent to Marion Scott on 3 August 1915 and published in *The Royal College of Music Magazine* Vol. XII, No. 1 (Christmas Term 1915); this was the first time that a poem of Gurney's had appeared in print. **p.3 Strange Service:** (*ibid.*) sent to Marion Scott on 27 July 1916. **p.4 Bach and the Sentry:** (*ibid.*) sent to Marion Scott on 8 November 1916. **p.5 Song:** (*ibid.*) sent to Marion Scott on 18 January 1917. **p.5 Pain:** (*ibid.*) sent to Marion Scott on 7 February 1917. The second of five *Sonnets 1917 (To the Memory of Rupert Brooke).* **p.6 Ballad of the Three Spectres:** (*ibid.*) sent to Marion Scott on 15 February 1917. **p.7 To the Prussians of England:** sent to Marion Scott on 12 October 1917. **p.7 'My heart makes songs on lonely roads':** sent to F. W. Harvey in February 1918 but dated November 1917. **p.8 Photographs:** (*War's Embers*, 1919) sent to Marion Scott on 20 January 1918 but dated December 1917. The 'Two Scots Lads' may be the Scottish engineers with whom Gurney worked on the 'soft job' during Christmas 1916. **p.9 To his Love:** (*ibid.*) sent to Marion Scott on 20 January 1918. **p.9 Above Ashleworth:** sent to Marion Scott on 12 March 1918 but dated February 1918. **p.10 Turmut-hoeing:** (*War's Embers*, 1919) manuscript dated August 1918. A turmut is a turnip. **p.11 Toussaints:** (*ibid.*) manuscript dated September 1918. The poem is dedicated to John Wilton Haines (1876–1960), solicitor, poet and a close friend of Gurney and Edward Thomas. **p.12 Equal Mistress:** manuscript on loose sheets of paper *c.* February 1919. Published in *Music and Letters* Vol. I, No. 4 (October 1920). **p.12 The Valley:** (red hardcover 'Aylecliffe' notebook, *c.* March 1919.) 'Kyrie Eleison and Gloria, | Credo, Jubilate,

Magnificat' are all items of the Ordinary of the Mass. **p.13 The Compan-
ions:** (*ibid.*). **p.14 'When from the curve of the wood's edge':**
manuscript on loose sheet. A later typescript has a note by Marion Scott:
'This poem was written in 1919 or 1920 by Ivor Gurney | and he gave me a
copy but would not let it be published in | the R.C.M. Magazine because he
said it was too intimate.'

II. 1920–September 1922

p.15 Western Sky-Look: undated manuscript on loose sheet. Published
as 'Western Sky' in *The Nation and Athenaeum*, Vol. 29, No. 21 (20 August
1921). Ferdinand Magellan (*c.* 1480–1521), John Cabot (*c.* 1474–1557)
and Francis Drake (1540–1596) are all notable naval explorers. **p.6 The
Change:** black hardcover exercise book inscribed 'I B Gurney | 1 Westfield
Terrace | Longford | Gloucester' in use between 1921 and 1922. The words
'the act of writing is a distraction in madness' are written on the
penultimate page. **p.6 The Songs I had:** (*ibid.*) published in *Music and
Letters* Vol. XIX, No. 1 (January 1938) as part of the symposium on
Gurney's life and work. **p.7 London Dawn:** (*ibid.*) 'Lockhart's' is a
restaurant or tea shop. Blackfriars Lane is particularly significant for
Gurney, being the area of London where Ben Jonson lived. **p.17 Generations:** (*ibid.*). **p.18 Moments:** (*ibid.*). **p.18 When I am covered:** (*ibid.*).
p.19 Longford Dawns: (*ibid.*). **p.19 Saturday's comings:** (*ibid.*). **p.20
Had I a song:** (*ibid.*). **p.20 What evil coil:** (*ibid.*). **p.20 The hoe scrapes
earth:** (*ibid.*) published in *Music and Letters* Vol. XIX, No. 1 (January 1938)
as part of the symposium on Gurney's life and work. **p.21 Defiance:**
undated manuscript on loose sheet. Dorothy Gurney typed out similar
manuscripts in early 1922 and selections from these were submitted to
Sidgwick & Jackson in May as *80 poems*. Published in the *London Mercury*
Vol. XXX, No. 175 (January 1934). **p.21 Encounters:** undated manuscript on page torn from exercise book. Again, similar manuscripts were
used to create *80 poems*. Published in the *London Mercury* Vol. VI, No. 36
(October 1922). **p.22 Lovely playthings:** (*ibid.*) there is also a Dorothy
Gurney typescript of this text. **p.22 Rainy Midnight:** Dorothy Gurney
typescript. Elvers is a young eel, considered a delicacy in Gloucester. **p.23
Personages:** (*80 poems*, 1922) Queen Deirdre is an Irish mythological
character and the subject of a 1907 play by W. B. Yeats. Rosalind is a
character in Shakespeare's *As You Like It.* **p.23 April Gale:** (*ibid.*). **p.24**

Common Things: (*ibid.*) a helve is the handle of a tool or weapon. **p.24 The Road:** (*ibid.*) shorter version published in *The Spectator* Vol. 130, No. 4787 (31 March 1923). **p.27 The Square Thing:** (*ibid.*) St Mary's church in Norton has a distinctive medieval perpendicular tower. **p.27 Apprentices:** (*ibid.*). **p.28 Time to Come:** (*ibid.*). **p.29 Generations:** (*ibid.*) John Gaunt is a character from Shakespeare's *Richard II*. Shallow appears in *Henry IV, Part II.* **p.29 The Garden:** (*ibid.*). **p.29 Daily:** (*ibid.*) published as 'Old Tale' in the *London Mercury* Vol. IX, No. 51 (January 1924). **p.30 Darkness has cheating swiftness:** green hardcover exercise book inscribed 'the Note book | (between music makings) | of Ivor Gurney | 1921–1922. | corrected | Feb 1925. | Ivor Gurney.' This is the uncorrected 1922 text. Slightly different version published in the *London Mercury* Vol. XXIX, No. 170 (December 1933). **p.30 The Soaking:** (*ibid.*) published in the *London Mercury* Vol. XXIX, No. 171 (January 1934). **p.30 Tobacco:** pink, marbled-effect hardcover exercise book with 'instead of a home | I require death' written on the inside of the back cover; in use by mid 1922. Germanicus Julius Caesar (15 BC–AD19) was a Roman emperor who, in AD14, quelled mutinous legions stationed in Germany. **p.32 Half dead:** (*ibid.*). **p.33 Near Vermand:** (*ibid.*). **p.33 Drachms + Scruples:** (*ibid.*) published in the *London Mercury* Vol. XXX, No. 178 (August 1934). Drachms and scruples are jewellers' weights. **p.34 Stars Sliding:** (*ibid.*) published in the *London Mercury* Vol. XXX, No. 178 (August 1934). **p.34 Brown earth Look:** (*ibid.*). **p.35 When March blows:** (*ibid.*) published in the *London Mercury* Vol. XXIX, No. 171 (January 1934). **p.35 The Miracles:** (*ibid.*). **p.35 Robecq again:** (*ibid.*) published in the *London Mercury* Vol. XXIX, No. 171 (January 1934). **p.36 Kettle-song:** (*ibid.*). **p.36 Larches:** (*ibid.*) the Scottish poet Robert Burns (1759–96) and the biblical King David, soldier and musician, are mentioned here. **p.37 Mist on Meadows:** (*ibid.*). **p.37 Old thought:** (*ibid.*) published in the *London Mercury* Vol. XXIX, No. 170 (December 1933). **p.38 Hedges:** (*ibid.*) 'Bread and cheese' is the country name for a wild flower, probably Common Mallow. **p.38 The High Hills have a bitterness:** (*ibid.*) published in the *London Mercury* Vol. XXX, No. 175 (May 1934). **p.39 Leckhampton Chimney has fallen down:** (*ibid.*) Leckhampton Chimney, also known as Devil's Chimney, is a prominent pillar of stone deliberately carved out on the sheer cliff edge at Leckhampton Hill by 19th-century quarrymen. **p.39 When the body might free:** (*ibid.*) published in the *London Mercury* Vol. XXIX, No. 171 (January 1934). **p.40 Up there:** (*ibid.*). **p.40 Midnight:** (*ibid.*). **p.41 Sonnet. September 1922:** loose undated sheet.

III. October 1922–December 1924

p.42 To God: group of poems written in pencil on lined paper torn from a block, some marked 'Barnwood House'. **p.42 There is a man:** (*ibid.*) Gurney repeatedly made appeals to the London Metropolitan Police, whom he believed to be involved in his continued confinement in some way. **p.43 The Incense Bearers:** (*ibid.*). **p.44 A wish:** written in pencil on the same paper as the Barnwood group but marked 'Stone House'. **p.45 Old Times:** similar in appearance to 'A wish'. **p.45 On Somme:** (*ibid.*). **p.46 The Escape:** corrected typescript of poem from pink marbled-effect notebook, *c.* October 1923. **p.46 Thoughts of New England:** *London Mercury* Vol IX, No. 51 (January 1924). J. C. Squire's source for this – corrected typescripts from the green exercise book – is no longer extant. The Old Raven Tavern is an inn in Gloucester which was owned by the Hoare family in the 17th century, some of whom emigrated to America with the Pilgrim Fathers. The *Citizen* is a Gloucester newspaper. Henry David Thoreau (1817–62), Oliver Wendell Holmes (1809–1894) and James Russell Lowell (1819–91) were American poets and essayists, whilst Nathaniel Hawthorne (1804–64) was an American novelist. William I spent Christmas 1085 in Gloucester, holding court and planning the preparation of the Domesday Book. Abana and Pharpar are biblical rivers. George Washington (1732–99) and Abraham Lincoln (1800–65) were American presidents, and the references to Wilderness, Richmond and Chattanooga relate to scenes of battle during the American Civil War. Generals Grant (1822–85) and Lee (1807–70) were opponents in the conflict. **p.49 New Year's Eve:** (*ibid.*) a limber is the detachable front of a gun carriage. **p.49 Smudgy Dawn:** (*ibid.*). **p.50 Brimscombe:** (*ibid.*). **p.50 Cut Flowers:** written in pencil on lined paper; undated but in handwriting very similar to the Barnwood group of poems. Possibly early 1923. **p.52 By Severn:** typescript volume entitled 'REWARDS OF WONDER | Poems of Cotswold, France, London. | – by – | IVOR GURNEY'. This collection was assembled from the corrected green and pink exercise book typescripts; these were then altered further. It can be provisionally dated to August 1923, when Gurney mentions it by name in a number of asylum appeals. 'Oriana' is one of the names applied to Elizabeth I by her poetic contemporaries. **p.53 Laventie:** (*ibid.*) a 'minnie werfer', literally meaning bomb thrower, is a German trench-mortar. 'Machonchie, Paxton, Tickler, and Gloucester Stephens; | Fray Bentos, Spillers and Baker, Odds' are all food rations allotted to soldiers in the trenches; 'Machonchie', for example, was a tinned meat and vegetable mixture and 'Stephens' was a brand of jam made in Gloucester. **p.54 Canadians:** (*ibid.*) Stewart White

(1873–1946) was a Canadian author of novels depicting rugged outdoor life. **p.55 Of Cruelty:** (*ibid.*). **p.56 The Cloud:** (*ibid.*). **p.56 Kilns:** (*ibid.*). **p.58 First Time In:** (*ibid.*) 'David of the white rock' and the 'Slumber Song' are folk songs. **p.58 La Gorgues:** (*ibid.*) the correct spelling is in fact La Gorgue but Gurney consistently spells it this way. **p.59 Blighty:** (*ibid.*). **p.60 Strange Hells:** (*ibid.*) 'Après la guerre fini' was a military song popular in the trenches, sung to the tune of 'The Bridges of Paris'. The reference to '12 inch – 6 inch and 18 pounders' describes sizes of guns and artillery. **p.61 The Comparison:** (*ibid.*) The Worcestershire and Hereford-shire Beacons are popular vantage points on the Malvern hills. **p.61 Crucifix Corner:** (*ibid.*) a 'crump' is the burst from a 5.9 inch shell, the nickname being derived from the sound it makes on landing. 'Happy we've been a'together' is a Scottish folk song. **p.62 I Saw England (July Night):** (*ibid.*) George Borrow (1803–81) was a novelist and essayist; Thomas Hardy (1840–1928) was a poet and novelist. **p.63 Poem For End:** (*ibid.*). **p.64 The Betrayal:** undated typescript set 'MISCELLANEOUS POEMS|BY| IVOR GURNEY'. Possibly assembled by Marion Scott in 1928 for the projected Gollancz edition of Gurney's poems. Placed here conjecturally. **p.64 Hell's Prayer:** (*ibid.*). **p.65 Masterpiece:** undated manuscript on loose sheets. Gurney's note at the bottom '*27th month*' dates this to around December 1924; he frequently dates his asylum manuscripts in this way, the first month being October 1922, the date of his committal. 'Weltmüth', or more properly, *Weltmut*, means World-courage. Sarsparilla is a cordial used as a tonic. Lyons and Lipton are tea manufacturers. **p.66 December 30th:** 'Miscellaneous Poems'.

IV. January 1925–April 1926

p.68 March: typescript collection 'THE THREEPENNY EXERCISE BOOK|of | IVOR GURNEY. | To | "HAWTHORNDEN"' dated 1 January 1925. 'Hawthornden' is one of Gurney's names for Annie Nelson Drummond, a pun on the name of Ben Jonson's Scottish friend, Drummond of Hawthorn-den and the Hawthornden poetry prize. **p.68 The Sea Borders:** (*ibid.*) **p.69 The Love Song:** (*ibid.*). **p.70 Snow:** (*ibid.*) actually dated 2 January 1925. **p.71 Thoughts on Beethoven:** green exercise book corrected in February 1925. Published in *Music and Letters* Vol. VII, No. 2 (April 1927). Ludwig van Beethoven (1770–1827) spent most of his life and eventually died in Vienna. **p.72 First poem:** another pink, marbled-effect hardcover exercise book inscribed ' "*The book of Five makings*" | Feb 1925. | (in torture) | *Ivor*

Gurney.' **p.72 Thoughts:** (*ibid.*) one of two versions with the same title. 'Voces Intimae' is a string quartet by Sibelius. The French writers mentioned are the critic Louis Petit de Julleville, the poet Pierre de Ronsard (1524–85) and Francis Jammes (1868–1938), poet and writer of short stories. Robert Bridges (1844–1930) was Poet Laureate from 1913 until his death. **p.73 Like Hebridean:** (*ibid.*) one of two versions. The other is called 'Hebridean'. **p.73 The Strange thing:** (*ibid.*) one of two versions. The other is called 'A Strange thing'. Wattignies, south of Lille, was the scene of Jourdan's victory over the Austrians in October 1793. **p.74 Epitaph on a Young Child:** (*ibid.*). **p.75 Christopher Marlowe:** (*ibid.*). **p.76 Song of Autumn:** (*ibid.*). **p.76 The Last of the book:** (*ibid.*). **p.77 Butchers and Tombs:** typescript collection '*MEMORIES OF HONOUR.* | INFANTRY POEMS | – and – | OF THE STATE OF NEW YORK | Ivor Gurney, | *March, 1925.*' **p.78 Serenade:** (*ibid.*) *Ein Heldenleben* – 'a hero's life' – is the symphonic poem by Richard Strauss (1864–1949), first performed in 1899. **p.78 Don Juan in Hell:** (*ibid.*). **p.79 The Bohemians:** (*ibid.*) 'putties are ankle strappings worn by soldiers. **p.79 To Long Island First:** typescript collection '*POEMS TO THE STATES* | (*The United States of North America*). | *Ivor Gurney,* | *March, 1925.*' **p.80 The New Poet:** typescript collection '*SIX POEMS* | – of the – | *NORTH AMERICAN STATES.* | *Ivor Gurney.* | War Poet.' It actually contains eight poems, one of which is dated 1 April 1925. **p.81 Signallers:** (*ibid.*) 'skilly' is a thin broth or gruel. **p.81 It is near Toussaints:** part of a set of manuscripts on pages torn from an exercise book, some of which are sources for 'Best poems' and thus *c.* November 1925. Hilaire Belloc (1870–1953) was an essayist, poet and travel writer. St Michael's and the 'Maries' – St Mary de Lode, St Mary de Crypt, St Mary Magdalene – are ancient churches in Gloucester. **p.82 Song:** blue 'Marspen' exercise book used as a source for 'Best poems' *c.* November 1925. **p.83 The Mangel-bury:** (*ibid.*) a 'Mangel-bury' is a thatched heap of mangold-wurzels, root vegetables farmed to feed cattle. **p.84 'They have left me little indeed':** (*ibid.*). **p.84 The Depths:** another pink 'Student' exercise book, containing poems dated February 1926. **p.85 Early Winter:** (*ibid.*). **p.85 Farewell:** undated manuscript on loose sheet in very similar handwriting to 'Best poems'. The request to type is actually written down the right hand side of the page. **p.86 The Sudden Storm:** brown and blue marbled-effect hardcover exercise book inscribed 'Best poems *of New* | *England* | *of City of Gloucester* | *of Embankment* | *of Aldgate* | *City of Bristol* | *Tewkesbury.* | Ivor Gurney. *Others.* | *Carnegie Award, 1922–24* | *London Mercury, 1922–3* | – 4. | *2/5 Gloucesters, 1915–1918* | *First war poet.* | (He does truly | believe)'. Completed between November 1925 and April

1926. **p.87 Ben Jonson:** (*ibid.*). **p.88 Of Grandcourt:** (*ibid.*). **p.89 The Silent One:** (*ibid.*). **p.89 Elizabethans:** (*ibid.*) Francis Beaumont (1584–1616) and John Fletcher (1579–1625) collaborated on a number of plays including *The Maid's Tragedy* and *Philaster* (both 1611). *The Roaring Girl* (1611) is the comedy by Thomas Decker (1570?–1632) and Thomas Middleton (1570?–1627). The other play is probably *The Fair Maid of the West, or a Girl Worth Gold* (1631) by Thomas Heywood (1574?–1641). Professor Henry Morley (1838–1933) was a prolific compiler of anthologies of English literature. Robert Greene (1560–92) was a poet, playwright and pamphleteer. **p.90 Portrait of a Coward:** (*ibid.*). **p.91 War books:** (*ibid.*).

V. September 1926–March 1929

p.92 the Shelter from the Storm: group of manuscripts on loose sheets with 'Mimosa' watermark, some dated September 1926. **p.92 I read now so:** (*ibid.*). **p.93 Near Spring:** similar group of manuscripts on loose sheets, some also dated September 1926. **p.94 Sea-Marge:** (*ibid.*). **p.94 the Bridge:** (*ibid.*). **p.95 the dancers:** similar group of manuscripts on loose sheets, with various dates from 1926. **p.95 Musers afar will say:** (*ibid.*). **p.96 the Pedlars Song:** (*ibid.*) dated 'Nov. 1926'. **p.97 I would not rest:** (*ibid.*). **p.97 'Soft rain beats upon my windows':** undated manuscript on loose sheet. A typescript version notes that this was 'written at Dartford, probably about 1926 or 1927'. **p.98 The Wind:** written on the back of an Oxford University Press letterhead dated 6 March 1929. Signed '*Valentine Fane*' by Gurney; he frequently used such names on his later manuscripts.

Glossary

AENEAS   see *Virgil*

AESCHYLUS   Athenian tragic poet (525–456BC). Gurney read and admired John Stuart Blackie's translation of *The Lyrical Dramas of Aeschylus* (1906) in the trenches

ALDGATE   London street and principal east gate of the city

'THE ALCHEMIST'   see *Jonson*

BILLET   military term for place of rest assigned to soldiers

BLIGHTY   soldiers' slang for home or England. Also the name given to a wound that ensured a return to Blighty, hence the term 'lucky blighter'

CANTERBURY   see *Marlowe*

'CAPTAINS COURAGEOUS'   see *Kipling*

CHAPMAN, GEORGE   poet and dramtist (1599?–1634?), chiefly known for his translations of Homer's *Iliad* (1611) and *Odyssey* (1614–15). Irus is a beggar in the latter

CROSS   see *Four ways*

CRUCIFIX CORNER   a prominent landmark in Neuve-Chappelle, so called because the large crucifix that stood there remained intact despite heavy bombardment

'DRUM TAPS'   see *Whitman*

DUG-OUT, DUGOUT   military term for a roofed shelter in the trenches

ESTAMINET   Frence café selling food and alcohol

'EVANGELINE'   see *Longfellow*

FATIGUES   a soldier's non-military duties, such as digging, wire-mending or food preparation

'FAUSTUS'   see *Marlowe*

FIRST LINE   see *the Line*

FLEET   appropriately for Gurney, both river and street in London, leading up Ludgate Hill to St Paul's Cathedral

FORD, JOHN   dramatist (1586?–1640). Little is known about his life but he is most famous for *'Tis Pity She's a Whore* (1631)

FOUR WAYS   until 1751, a medieval cross stood at the centre of Gloucester where its four principal roads – Northgate, Southgate, Eastgate and Westgate Streets – meet

FRONT LINE   see *the Line*

GLOUCESTER'S ABBEY   the site of Gloucester Cathedral was occupied during the Dark Ages by a monastery ruled by Kyneburg, sister of King Ofrich. After the Norman Conquest it became the church of St Peter. Gurney's use of these alternative names for the cathedral suggests his awareness of historical survivals

HOMER, HOMERIC   see *Chapman*

'HUNDRED PIPERS AND A''   Scottish folk tune, used as a marching song

ILIAD   see *Chapman*

IRUS   see *Chapman*

JOHNSON   Gurney's misspelling of Jonson

JONSON, BEN   poet and dramatist (1572–1637) whose best known plays include *The Alchemist* (1610) and *Bartholomew Fair* (1614). His stubborn belief in his superior talent and his military service in Flanders may explain why Gurney regarded him as a 'Master'

KINEBURGH'S COTTAGE   see *Gloucester's Abbey*

KIPLING, RUDYARD   poet, novelist and author of short stories (1865–1936) whose *Captains Courageous* (1897), a novel of sea adventure, and *Puck of Pook's Hill* (1906) – 'Sussex tales out of Roman heights callen' – were much admired by Gurney. In *Something of Myself* (1936), Kipling describes his experiences in New England during 1892

'LEAVES OF GRASS'   see *Whitman*

THE LINE   a military term describing the arrangement of trenches on the Western Front. Troops spent between three and seven days in the front or first line trench, which directly faced the enemy. They would then withdraw to the support line trench for a similar period of time and then go back to the reserve line trench. After this, a week was spent 'on Rest' before returning to the front

LONGFELLOW, HENRY WADSWORTH   American essayist and poet (1807–82). *Evangeline* (1847) is a narrative poem set in the early years of the American nation

LONG ISLAND   see *Whitman*

MARLOWE, CHRISTOPHER   Canterbury-born poet and dramatist (1564–93) who was murdered in mysterious circumstances. His plays include *Tamburlaine* (1587) and *Doctor Faustus* (1601)

MARSTON, JOHN   dramatist (1575?–1634), author of *The Malcontent* (1604)

NICHOLAS   a church of Norman origin in the centre of Gloucester.

OUR GREAT BEN   see *Jonson*

PAUL, PAUL'S, PAULS   St Paul's Cathedral in London, reconstructed by Sir Christopher Wren (1632–1723) after the Great Fire of London

PETER'S ABBEY   see *Gloucester's Abbey*

RESERVE   see *the Line*

SHIRLEY, JAMES   dramatist (1596–1666). Author of comedies, tragedies and masques

SQUELE, WILL   'a Cotswold man' in Shakespeare's *Henry IV*, Part II

STRAFE   sustained bombardment by rifle or artillery, from the German *Gott strafe England* – 'God punish England'

SUSSEX TALES   see *Kipling*

'TAMBURLAINE'   see *Marlowe*

'THIS COMPOST'   see *Whitman*

THOMAS, EDWARD   poet and essayist (1878–1917). Gurney's friend John Haines knew him well and Gurney considered himself an 'E.T. enthusiast'

TOUSSAINTS   All Saints' Day, 1 November

ULYSSES   Latin name for Odysseus, the mythical king who spent twenty years returning home after the Trojan wars, many of them at sea

VEREY, VEREY LIGHTS   flares fired from a special pistol, used for signalling at night or for illuminating the enemy's position

VIRGIL   Roman poet (70–19BC). Gurney responded to the mixture of poetry, war, wandering and return in his *Aeneid* and the experiences of its eponymous hero

WHITMAN, WALT   American poet (1819–92) born on Long Island whose works include *Drum Taps* (1865) and 'This Compost', both of which were included in *Leaves of Grass* (final edition 1891).

WREN   see *Paul*

Everyman's Poetry

Titles available in this series **all at £1.00**

William Blake
ed. Peter Butter
0 460 87800 X

Robert Burns
ed. Donald Low
0 460 87814 X

Samuel Taylor Coleridge
ed. John Beer
0 460 87826 3

Thomas Gray
ed. Robert Mack
0 460 87805 0

Ivor Gurney
ed. George Walter
0 460 87797 6

George Herbert
ed. D. J. Enright
0 460 87795 X

Robert Herrick
ed. Douglas Brooks-Davies
0 460 87799 2

John Keats
ed. Nicholas Roe
0 460 87808 5

**Henry Wadsworth
Longfellow**
ed. Anthony Thwaite
0 460 87821 2

John Milton
ed. Gordon Campbell
0 460 87813 1

Edgar Allan Poe
ed. Richard Gray
0 460 87804 2

Poetry Please!
Foreword by Charles
Causley
0 460 87824 7

Alexander Pope
ed. Douglas Brooks-Davies
0 460 87798 4

Lord Rochester
ed. Paddy Lyons
0 460 87819 0

Christina Rossetti
ed. Jan Marsh
0 460 87820 4

William Shakespeare
ed. Martin Dodsworth
0 460 87815 8

Alfred, Lord Tennyson
ed. Michael Baron
0 460 87802 6

R. S. Thomas
ed. Anthony Thwaite
0 460 87811 5

Walt Whitman
ed. Ellman Crasnow
0 460 87825 5

Oscar Wilde
ed. Robert Mighall
0 460 87803 4